Life from the Press Box

Life from the Press Box

FORTY YEARS WITH THE MUSTACHE GANG,
O.J., JOHN MADDEN, THE BIG UNIT,
SWEET LOU, JUNIOR GRIFFEY AND ICHIRO...

Jim Street

LIFE FROM THE PRESS BOX

iUniverse books may be ordered through booksellers or by contacting:

iUniverse
1663 Liberty Drive
Bloomington, IN 47403
www.iuniverse.com
1-800-Authors (1-800-288-4677)

ISBN: 978-1-4917-4537-3 (sc)
ISBN: 978-1-4917-4538-0 (hc)
ISBN: 978-1-4917-4536-6 (e)

Library of Congress Control Number: 2014917543

Printed in the United States of America.

iUniverse rev. date: 10/02/2014

Contents

Foreword

B ack in the corner of the old *Seattle Times* sports department sometime in the late 1980s, one of the sportswriters cut out and taped a quote on his desk that no doubt another writer had expressed.

It went something like, "Sportswriting is the best kind of ordinary life."

That resonated with me, because we, as the writers of sports, always seem to have an identity crisis. What do we really do? What's our role? We certainly aren't athletes—that's obvious when you take a glance at the press-box chow line. Yet our names and reputations are on the line every day; we have to perform, we have to entertain, and we can't make mistakes, because everyone will see them.

We also aren't fans. No cheering in the press box, no wearing of the team colors, no face painting. We are somewhere in between, literally—not back in the stands but also not on the playing fields, shadow figures huddling in the overhanging press boxes, always second-guessing.

Most of the time, we simply feel like grunts tediously transcribing notes; dealing with unrelenting deadlines and hyper-competitive rival reporters; and suffering through bad meals, late flights, and clueless editors.

Yet we must be having so much fun in our perceived parasitical roles, most fans believe, because we get into games free and have access to the clubhouse and the athletes. As one of my friends frequently used to ask me, "Did you go to play land today?"

But sportswriting is not a pastime or pursuit; it's our *job*. Our responsibility is to remain dispassionate, to cover the events without prejudice or partiality. We're not part of anyone's team. We're simply among a select group of individuals entrusted with providing a clear, reasoned assessment of what just happened. That makes us unique.

This is the kind of so-called ordinary life that Jim Street gravitated to at a young age, turning his passions into the best kind of extraordinary career. He's always had a love for baseball and a talent for expressing himself in words. For nearly four decades, he found a way to draw them together and, in the process, as he details in his book, has dealt with dynasties, tragedies, controversies, legends, and imbeciles.

Our friendship goes back more than three decades to when Jim and I both worked in the Bay Area. Our paths didn't cross often, as he was a writer for the *San Jose Mercury-News* and I was an editor at the *San Francisco Examiner*. But we did share some of the same experiences, either covering or writing about such notable events as Dwight's Flight, the 49ers' 1980 last-minute victory over Dallas that sent them to their first Super Bowl (in Detroit in 1981), and a shared earthquake or two.

In 1985, I moved to Seattle to be part of the *Seattle Times'* Mariners baseball coverage. Jim moved up eight months later to become the Mariners beat reporter for the *Seattle Post-Intelligencer.* For most of the next two decades, we were healthy competitors.

By healthy I mean we kept it professional, not personal. One of the negative by-products of sportswriting is that it's hard to maintain friendships when we're always trying to knock each other's heads off. You want to beat the competition every day on every story. That's in our DNA. There's a need and a pressure to be first. The readers generally don't care, but we do. That's how we keep score. We want to win as much as the players we cover. We're competitive. We're tenacious. If we weren't, we wouldn't be in those positions.

That kind of atmosphere can engender jealousy and backstabbing. There are legendary stories passed down in our business about sportswriters in various cities who wouldn't speak to each other for years, even decades, and avoided sharing cabs or lunch tables because of this profession's scoop mentality.

Jim Street played it straight, as professional as he could be. Both of us have dropped a scoop or two on the other—although Jim's well ahead on that scorecard. Yet when he had a significant story ahead of the rest of us, it was not in his character to boast or rub it in.

That's a rare quality, because the dirty little secret about sportswriters is they generally react quite strangely when scooped. In most other professions, when there's an elephant in the room, there is an acknowledgment of its presence. Not necessarily in the press box. Many times, when one of the writers has a scoop that day, it's greeted with a cacophony of silence. Privately, the other writers will claim various reasons for not having gotten it first—their editors held it; or it's unimportant; or they go for the full Fox News treatment and deny, condemn, or ignore.

When he was on the other side, on those rare occasions when I had a story first, Jim wouldn't hesitate to recognize it. One of the hardest things for a sportswriter to say to another sportswriter is "Good job." Jim has no problem with that kind of compliment, a testament to his professionalism and to his personal graciousness.

What has contributed to Jim's success and longevity in the profession—as well as our friendship—is his humor. He understands that we're not war reporters. We're not covering nuclear disarmament treaties or criminal trials. We cover games. We talk to more than our share of self-possessed cretins and then try to assemble a readable quote. Jim always saw and sought the humor in those conversations and conveyed it in his stories—as well as this book.

There was one postgame session in Texas, I remember, when Mariners reliever Shigetoshi Hasegawa went through a long, elaborate, hard-to-follow explanation to the media of why he had been ineffective that evening. As soon as he was done, Shiggy said, "Do you know what I mean?" Jim responded, "I don't have a clue what you just said."

We both prefer a light touch first over nuts and bolts. We have a similar sense of humor, but Jim's wit is sharper and quicker. You can't spend much time with him without cackling at his witticisms, his turns of phrase, and his crazy stories, many of which he relates here.

There also are plenty more stories that he left out, such as his touching narration of the princess nightstand episode or our wild adventure hanging out with Mariners coach Matt Sinatro and manager

Lou Piniella at Lou's Kansas City restaurant. Those will be in his sequel, perhaps.

It was an eventful time for the Mariners and Seattle sports during those years that we covered. The club never had a winning season for its first fifteen seasons, not until 1991. But after Piniella arrived in 1993, everything changed. Under Lou, the Mariners went to the playoffs four times—in 1995, 1997, 2000, and 2001. During that stretch, Junior Griffey put together a Hall-of-Fame career with clutch home runs, his eight-home-runs-in-eight-games record, his back-to-back fifty-six-home-run seasons, and his spectacular catches.

We witnessed one of baseball's greatest in-season comebacks in 1995 when the Mariners, trailing the Angels by twelve and a half games in early August, caught them. Then Randy Johnson was spectacular in a one-game playoff victory over the Angels to advance the Mariners to the postseason for the first time. In the first round, the Mariners came back from two games down to beat the Yankees, three games to two, on the greatest clutch hit in club history, Edgar Martinez's two-run eleventh-inning double.

We saw the emergence of Alex Rodriguez's enormous talent and ego. We saw the remarkable 2001 season in which the Mariners won a record 116 games led by MVP Japanese import Ichiro, the Sultan of Slap. It didn't take long before Jim recognized and called out Ichiro's arrogance and his wanton mistreatment of the media. Even if Ichiro is a superstar and future Hall of Famer, Jim wouldn't take any crap from him.

Jim also always seemed just a half step ahead of everyone else. Beyond the game stories, how we, as beat reporters, separated ourselves was with our daily notebooks. We were in a constant search for the lead item, something no one else had, a miniscoop. There was the time before a game I saw Jim talking to a couple of Latin players and wondered why only to read in his notebook that a storm had torn through their islands and he was getting their reaction. Another time I might see him talking to a reserve player for reasons unknown only to find out that player once had been a teammate of a player traded that day—little things. He'd beat you with pinpricks.

Sometimes we even came up with the same idea, like the time we both covered a Mariners game from our hotel rooms. Toronto's Skydome opened in 1989, that retractable-roof ballpark that has a hotel all along the outfield upper deck. We both thought how novel it would be to cover it from there. Not so novel, however, if both of us thought of it. Without mentioning it to each other beforehand, he had settled into his right-field upper-deck suite for the game, and I was looking out the window in my left-field upper-deck suite.

This book is remarkable for the relative ease and quickness with which it came together over just a couple of months. I'm amazed how Jim has been able to recall the years, the characters, and the situations of his working life. It has brought back plenty of memories, some wonderful, some I'd like to forget, from a time when newspapers mattered. Things have changed. It's a different era with new parameters. One day our grandchildren might ask, "What's a newspaper?"

Jim Street played a significant role in that bygone era, a vital and talented sportswriter during the Mariners' brief glory years and a national president of the Baseball Writers' Association of America during baseball's steroid era.

Throughout, he was a professional, which is the highest compliment I can give. He did a good job.

—Bob Sherwin

Introduction

An e-mail from my nephew Robbie Street in mid-October started a project that would take several months and about 60,000 words to complete.

Robbie wanted to know if there were three versions of the Oakland Athletics' 1973 World Series ring. As a reporter covering the A's during the first Athletics dynasty (1972–1974), I had received a ring from owner Charles O. Finley each year.

As far as I knew, there was only one version—the one I had—and it did not have a diamond in it. It didn't even have a zircon like the '72 ring for the nonplayers and, in some cases, seldom-used reserves. Finley got in hot water for that one, and MLB Commissioner Bowie Kuhn told him to replace the fake diamonds with real ones.

My dad wore the ring I received for the '73 Series for more than thirty-five years, and when his ring finger became too thin for the ring to stay on, he handed it over to Lary, one of my three brothers. He currently wears it with pride. I wear the '72 ring, and my son, Scott, has the '74 World Series ring.

Robbie also mentioned in the e-mail that if I hadn't thought about it before, I should consider writing a book about my career. If nothing else, it would give my grandchildren some insight into the life their grandpa lived. I had no plans to write such a book, but I thought about it and decided to go for it.

It was a good idea to do this project now rather than waiting until my brain was mush. The book came together much more easily than I expected. Memories and stories dating to 1963, when I was a senior at Butte Valley High School, came rushing back as though they had happened a few days before.

While I was sending in the year-by-year chapters, Robbie was editing the results into book form. It seemed to Lary, Robbie, and me to turn out extremely well. Little did I know that Robbie was learning how he could publish the results of this project for our family and friends.

My goal was to explain what it was like being a sportswriter traveling around the country to watch sporting events. It was a burden on my family, no doubt, but absence made my heart grow fonder of the people I cared the most about.

I feel lucky to have covered several World Series and All-Star Games, the first World Baseball Classic, two Super Bowls, four Rose Bowls, and the Kentucky Derby, along with the men's and women's US Open golf tournaments. It was quite a journey, to say the least. I had more fun than I ever could have imagined and met some wonderful people along the way.

Big thanks to Robbie for suggesting the project and spending so much of his time putting it together. Thanks also to my super wife, Becky, who put up with the time I spent in the man cave working on the book. She also came up with the book's name. Her patience is just one of her many virtues. Thanks also to my brother Lary, who painstakingly read through each chapter correcting spelling errors, and to Bob Sherwin for his input on finalizing the project.

I learned early in my career that *fairness* and *accuracy* are two of the most important words of my profession. There are two sides to every story, and you must hear both sides in order to determine where the truth lies beyond the hurt. I hope all of my children, including my stepson Brad, and all of the children they produce get a chance to read this book. But most of all, I hope the family myths that have been around for years will be cleared up.

Chapter 1

1963–1971: Choosing a Career, Going to War

I decided at a young age, probably around sixteen or seventeen years old, that I was going to become a high-school baseball coach. I had absolutely no interest in being anything other than a physical education teacher and baseball coach. That combination would be the ticket to the life I wanted. After all, I slept, drank, and ate baseball.

But as a senior at Butte Valley High School, my varsity basketball coach, Lyle Chambers, suggested that I fill the one class period I had open with something called journalism. A small group of us in the brand-new class would cover various beats for the local weekly newspaper, the *Butte Valley Star*. I was assigned the sports beat, and it was love at first write. I covered the Bulldogs' athletic endeavors during my final year in high school. Thanks to Sylvia Copeland, who put together an album for one of the recent BVHS reunions, I still have a copy of my first byline.

It was a bad story, but most of the stories were awful including those written by other journalism classmates. We were taught to report who, what, why, when, and where, avoiding *me, myself,* and *I* at all times. As a basketball and baseball player, it was very uncomfortable for me to include my contributions to a game, win or lose. But I must admit the time I scored twenty-seven points in a basketball game and had a four-for-four baseball game later in the school year were pretty cool.

Still uncertain about my career path beyond high school, I met with my senior advisor, Mrs. Marlyn Hines (who also was my English teacher). She asked me what I was going to do after graduation, and I told her I planned on going to College of the Siskiyous (COS) to become either a baseball coach and teacher or a sportswriter. My grades were not good enough to be accepted by a four-year college as a freshman. She suggested that I skip college altogether and try to get a job at the local lumber mill where my dad worked.

Fortunately, I did not accept her advice. Unfortunately, she passed away before I had a chance to thank her for giving me an "I'll show her!" mentality or tell her I had discovered that it isn't what you know that counts but what you do with what you know.

COS had a journalism department. Several students put out a weekly mimeographed newspaper that included a sports section. I became, I believe, the first sports editor in COS history. During my sophomore year, the *Eagle's Cry* came out in newspaper form and was published by the *Mount Shasta Herald*.

Following my sophomore year at COS, I was hired as an intern with the Klamath Falls, Oregon, *Herald and News,* covering everything from American Legion baseball to city council meetings. I preferred the baseball games despite the wishes of seasoned colleague Pati O'Connor. "Why do you want to cover sports when so many other things are much more important?" she kept asking me. To me, nothing was more important than a good sporting event, especially a baseball game.

The experience I gained at the *Herald and News* that summer was huge. I even sold my first story—to *Sport Magazine.* Klamath Union High School athlete Mike Keck was an all-state player in baseball, football, and basketball. He was considered the best overall athlete in the state of Oregon.

I wrote a story on Mike's athletic ability and sent it to the national magazine for consideration for its Teenage Athlete of the Month feature. Several days later, I received a letter from the publisher. He liked the story and included was a check for twenty-five dollars.

Mike and I remained friends until his tragic death in 1971. He was killed in a one-car traffic accident en route from his parents' home in Klamath Falls to Reno, Nevada, during a break in the basketball season at Oregon State. Two of Mike's OSU teammates in the car with him survived the deadly accident.

It was earlier, in 1964, when I began to realize that a guardian angel was looking over me.

During my sophomore year, the COS baseball team's final road trip of the season was to Yuba City, California. A couple of the players purchased some beer and took it to their motel room, which was next to the room Bill Newlun and I were sharing. A door connected the two rooms. At some point in the night, we were invited to join the party, accepted the invitation, and spent about five minutes in the room—long enough for me to take one sip of beer and chat a little before returning to our room.

Unbeknownst to me or Noodles, some of the furniture in the adjoining room was broken after we departed, and naturally, the motel owners were not pleased. They notified the college higher-ups, who notified head coach John Mazzei. He, in turn, invited his entire team for a meeting and said each one of us should own up to what we had done or else we would be suspended from school. The baseball season, meanwhile, ended with two games remaining on the schedule.

A few days later, I went to Coach Mazzei's house and told him exactly what I had done, explaining that I had no knowledge of the damage done to the motel furniture.

So much for being honest—I was suspended from school and forced to drop three classes, which prevented me from graduating with the rest of my classmates. Most of the team was suspended, and it became known as the COS Black Sox Scandal. I learned later that I was going to be selected as the most improved player on the team—perhaps because I hit the only home run of my career, against Napa JC, with my nine-month-old nephew Michael looking on from his stroller. I'm not sure, but I think he cheered and clapped his little hands!

It was in February of 1965 that I decided I wanted to be a sportswriter. My journalism instructor at COS, James Witherell, had entered one of my stories in a statewide junior college write-in contest. The winners were to be announced at the annual Junior College Journalism Conference in Palm Springs, California. For the first time, COS was represented as Witherell and three students, including me, traveled to Palm Springs. I received a second-place award—the only JC writer north of Los Angeles

County to win anything at the conference. Journalism became more to me than a word.

As it turned out, the suspension that forced me to return to COS for another semester was the best thing that happened to me.

During my sophomore year, I had applied to several California colleges and been accepted by Fresno State and Chico State. I was not accepted by my number-one choice, San Jose State, recognized as one of the top journalism schools in the country. I reapplied to SJS during my fifth semester at COS and was accepted.

I made it through SJS in two years, earning a bachelor's degree in journalism. I worked for the SJS student newspaper both years. My college baseball-playing career ended in San Jose. I was not nearly good enough to earn a spot on the team, but helping to publish a daily newspaper was time consuming. However, I did play semipro in the Bay Area on weekends. Lew Armistead, my fellow sports editor at the *Spartan Daily,* was the player/manager of the San Mateo team, and as much as I hated to see my college baseball career end, the more I wrote, the more I enjoyed it. I covered a plethora of sports—soccer, judo, track and field, basketball, and water polo—at SJS and graduated in January 1968.

Two weeks later, my world changed.

I was drafted into the army and sent to Ft. Lewis, Washington, for basic and advanced infantry training. I learned how to shoot and kill, neither of which had been high on my bucket list. Despite efforts to use my college degree—Oregon Senator Wayne Morse and Ross Game, an executive with the Scripps League Newspapers, which owned the *Herald and News,* wrote letters to military contacts at the Pentagon requesting that I be assigned to a public information office position—I remained a foot soldier.

In July 1968, I received my marching orders: report to the Oakland Army Base for assignment to the Ninth Infantry Division in Long Binh, Vietnam. Gulp. I had a two-week advance notice. My mom drove me to Medford, Oregon, for my flight to Oakland and told me several years later that she cried all the way back home to Dorris, unsure if she would ever see her second son alive again.

Upon arriving in Vietnam—the stench of burning human poop is forever etched into my sense of smell—the incoming troops went through a week of training to get acclimated to the tropical Southeast Asia weather, which was hot and humid. At the barracks I was assigned, I met an older guy who had been in the reserves. He explained that he had missed so many meetings that he had been activated and sent to Vietnam. He was not happy.

I explained how I had tried to get out of infantry and into public information, and he did me a huge favor by assigning me as the barracks guard. While everyone else was out in the training field, I made sure no one stole the barracks. He also pointed out the location of the public information office (nearby) and suggested that I go over there and request a transfer. Despite daily sojourns to the PIO office, there was no opening for me to fill, and I was assigned to an infantry unit that had basically been wiped out in a recent firefight.

I was on the back of a truck when, out of the blue, this dude came up and asked, "Is there a Private Street here?" I raised my hand, grabbed my stuff, and got off the truck. I had a new job—as a reporter for the *Old Reliable,* the Ninth Infantry Division newspaper. As I learned later, John Imbach, a reporter, wanted to go out on a mission. When he finally got his wish, he was told that he never ever should stand up when taking pictures during a firefight. The unit he was with got into a gun battle with the Viet Cong; he stood up to take a picture. He was shot and killed, the only member of the PIO unit to be killed during the Vietnam War. His death opened up a spot for me at the PIO, and I was reassigned.

Luckily, I returned from all the missions I went on while stationed in the Mekong Delta. That is not to say there wasn't at least one close call. While patrolling an area near the Mekong River, the group of about twelve soldiers I was with came under enemy fire. We all hit the deck. I heard a distinct crack above me that sounded like a brittle branch breaking and assumed it was a bullet passing over my head, possibly too close for comfort.

My job was to write about these missions. One time, an officer came up to me after such a mission and told me to write that fifteen

Viet Cong had been killed. I told him that I had been there and not a shot had been fired.

He said, "Soldier, write what I tell you to write!"

I wrote the story, minus a byline, and I am sure he received another medal. I knew then that the war was not what I had been led to believe during the eight-week training period at Ft. Lewis.

Fortunately, the experience I had while working on the Spartan Daily at SJS paid off, as I was able to assemble an eight-page newspaper each week. I became the assistant editor of the *Old Reliable* and moved into a barracks in Dong Tam, the new home of the Ninth Infantry Division, deep in the heart of the Mekong Delta.

The PIO personnel resided on the second floor of a two-story barracks. Members of South Vietnamese Army intelligence were on the first floor. "Incoming!" was a routine word. The Viet Cong would launch periodical mortar attacks.

On this particular night, or in the early hours of the morning, there was incoming, so we all rushed into the bunker beneath the barracks. The shelling eventually stopped, and it was clear to return to our bunks. I went to my bed, which I expected to be empty. It was not.

A South Vietnamese soldier had gotten confused, and instead of going to his bunk on the bottom floor, he had gone to mine in the second floor. He was either very drunk or very sleepy, and I could not get him to leave. I could have picked him up and thrown him downstairs but figured that wasn't a good idea.

My pals from the PIO found this very amusing. I was the only one not laughing. I eventually convinced the Vietnamese dude to get up, get out, and get into his own bed. War was hell.

One of my assignments was covering Bob Hope's annual Christmas trip to Vietnam, which included a stop at the Ninth Infantry Division headquarters in Dong Tam. His entourage of talent included Ann Margret, the Gold Diggers, and Les Brown & His Band of Renown.

It was a great show, and I felt honored to be the one writing the story. Several years later, when I was covering the Bing Crosby Pro-Am Golf Tournament, I was able to spend a few seconds with Mr. Hope and thank him for that December day in 1968. He was very gracious and seemed genuinely happy that I survived the war.

The *Old Reliable* was produced at the *Stars and Stripes* bureau in Tokyo, and for two months of my yearlong assignment in Vietnam, I was in Tokyo as the production editor.

I even had a tour guide during my temporary duty assignment in Tokyo—Susumu Fukatsu, a college student who had befriended Mike West, my predecessor.

Those were good times, and I even received the hazardous-duty pay that all troops received while in Vietnam. I never questioned it, especially after riding with some of those crazy-ass cab drivers in Tokyo.

Upon my return to 'Nam, I was assigned various duties, but mostly I remained in the much safer base camps at all times, writing stories from there. One of my final weeks was supposed to be spent in Sydney, Australia, on a rest and recuperation (R&R) sojourn that all troops received during the time in 'Nam. I never went. I was given the choice of 1) going to Australia for the R&R or 2) going home early. I was on the list of troops being sent back to the US as part of the first withdrawal from the Vietnam War in July of 1969. I chose option number two.

I returned to the US via an Air Force jet. We rode backward in a plane with no windows. We didn't care. After brief stopovers in Okinawa (engine trouble) and Honolulu (we were quarantined while there) we arrived at McChord Air Base near Ft. Lewis. The city of Seattle had prepared a welcome-home parade downtown. The streets were lined primarily with invisible people. It was not a popular war.

My parents were at the Klamath Falls airport to give a genuine welcome home, and I was able to thank my dad, up close and personal, for writing me a letter every day while I was in Vietnam. It was something far above the call of duty and something I would never, ever forget—not even to this day. The *Herald and News* had sent a reporter to the airport to greet the returning soldiers but did not know I was one of them.

The returnees were listed by state, so I was on the list of Californians. The other two were Oregonians. The reporter, whom I had worked with at the newspaper, was surprised to see me, to say the least. He later called my parents' home and invited me up to Klamath Falls for an interview.

I still had six months remaining on my two-year military commitment and was assigned to the Presidio of San Francisco. While preparing to leave Vietnam, we had been instructed to list three preferences for reassignment. The Presidio of San Francisco had been my first choice, followed by the Presidio of Monterey and Fort Ord. My new home was too good to be true. How sweet was that! My job: give guided tours of the Presidio, which was located on the doorstep of the Golden Gate Bridge.

Among the many perks of being in San Francisco was the proximity to some major newspapers in the Bay Area. I landed a part-time job at the *Oakland Tribune* working with the prep department on Tuesday and Friday nights—the busiest times for football and basketball.

I was hoping for full-time employment at the *Tribune* when I was discharged from the army in March 1970, but there were no openings in the sports department.

I could have returned to the *Herald and News* in Klamath Falls, but I had bigger ambitions. I checked with other Bay Area newspapers, including the *San Jose Mercury-News*. Several SJS grads worked at the paper including three in the sports department. Jeff Stockton, a former *Spartan Daily* sports editor, told me that one of the *Mercury-News* reporters would soon be leaving to take a job in Santa Monica, California, covering the Dodgers. Louie Duino, the sports editor, was nice enough to give me a job interview, although there were no jobs available. I explained during our meeting that I was aware that one of his reporters would soon be leaving and asked him please to keep me in mind when it happened.

A week later, in March of 1970 and shortly after my discharge from the army, Bill Miller left the *Mercury-News* for Santa Monica. I received a phone call from Louie, and he offered me a part-time job working three nights a week on preps. I had hoped for a full-time job but accepted the offer, and that was my work schedule for a little more than a year, until the summer of 1971.

Ignacio Lopez, a sports columnist for the *San Jose News,* attended spring training in Arizona that year and came down with an illness. He passed away in July, and Ignacio's columnist position went unfilled for about a month. John Lindblom, covering the Oakland Athletics at the time, accepted an offer to become the new news columnist. I was offered the position of Oakland Athletics beat writer for the remainder of the season with no promises beyond that season attached. I accepted the offer and took over the beat in August 1971. I had a full-time job. The A's had a sixteen-game lead and won the AL (American League) West by a wide margin before losing to the Orioles in the AL Championship Series. My work was deemed "good enough," and I remained on the A's beat.

At some point during the '71 season, Reggie Jackson gave me a nickname: "Quarterback." He recalled that the University of Texas had a quarterback named James Street who led the Longhorns to the national championship in 1969. The nickname has stuck ever since—at least in the Bay Area. I never met James Street the quarterback, but many years later I met his son, Huston, a pitcher for the Oakland Athletics.

My life with the Mustache Gang was assured for at least one more season. Life was good—really good!

Chapter 2

1972: Strike One

My first major-league spring training camp was crazy, to say the least. The good vibes created by the Athletics' first playoff appearance since the team moved from Kansas City prior to the 1968 season were short-lived.

The Athletics' camp opened in Mesa, Arizona, without Vida Blue, the twenty-four-game winner and the American League Cy Young Award winner. He was a holdout, rejecting owner Charles O. Finley's $63,000 contract offer. Vida had made less than $15,000 in 1971 and wanted to be compensated for his breakout '71 season.

Besides that, the collective basic agreement between players and owners expired after the '71 season, and camps opened without a deal in place. Almost every day that spring began with a phone call to Finley at his office in Chicago for an update on Blue. Charlie was cordial at times, gruff at other times, and downright rude on other occasions. But the phone calls continued.

Midway through camp, Finley made his annual pilgrimage to the desert, and the only thing anyone wanted to talk about was Vida. When will he sign? Will he sign? Finley arrived at the team's hotel headquarters in Phoenix; met late into the night with player rep Chuck Dobson; and, at around midnight, had the team's PR director call Ron Bergman (of the *Oakland Tribune*) and me for a press conference in the coffee shop at the hotel. We were the only Bay Area writers covering the team. It was almost 12:30 a.m. when we arrived.

Finley insisted that Dobson attend the press conference, so the four of us discussed the Vida Blue saga. It was not fun. Bergie and I returned to our respective rooms and wrote our stories—his for the afternoon *Tribune* and mine for the afternoon *San Jose News*.

A few days later, Bergman and I drove to Tucson for a Cactus League game. Afterward, Finley asked if he could hitch a ride back to Phoenix with us. I drove. Bergman rode shotgun. Finley was in the backseat.

As we approached the on-ramp to I-10 from Tucson to Phoenix, there was a young couple with their thumbs out. At Finley's urging, we stopped and offered them a lift. They accepted and climbed into the backseat with Charlie.

All of a sudden, Charlie took a copy of the latest issue of *Sports Illustrated* and turned to a story about Vida's holdout. He showed the story (and pictures) to the young couple and asked if they had ever heard of Vida. They hadn't. He also asked if they had heard of Charles Oscar Finley. They hadn't.

The remainder of the ride back to Phoenix was pretty quiet.

Training camp started and ended without Vida. The regular season didn't start on time either. The players walked out and stayed out for almost two weeks—from April 1 through April 13, 1972. For the first time in my life, I hated baseball.

I returned to San Jose, wrote some stories, and worked on the *Mercury-News* desk, which made me hate baseball even more.

The season finally started on April 15 against the Twins in Oakland. The A's won the game, 4–3, in eleven innings in front of a crowd of 9,912 fans. It would be one of the largest crowds of the early season as fans showed their anger over the strike. Fans gradually returned, and 37,444 attended the A's-White Sox game on May 27 at the Oakland Coliseum.

The Athletics drew 921,323 fans that season, the second-lowest total in the American League. Only three AL teams topped the 1 million mark. The payroll, "estimated" at $997,506, was by far the highest in the league, and why not? The A's were the best team in the major leagues.

That payroll eventually would include Vida's salary. He held out until May 2. Commissioner Bowie Kuhn interceded and, in the best interests of baseball, forced Finley to honor the final offer he made to Blue—a $50,000 base salary and $13,000 signing bonus. It was a hefty raise from the $14,500 Vida made in '71. The A's were in Boston when the signing occurred and already had opened up a comfortable lead in the AL West.

Finley spent another $7,500 in bonus money to the Mustache Gang.

Reggie Jackson reported to camp with a full-blown mustache, and Finley was not happy about it. He told manager Dick Williams to tell Reggie to shave it off. Reggie refused. But rather than start an in-house ruckus, Finley encouraged a couple of other players to grow one, figuring Jackson would shave off his mustache.

Several players including Catfish Hunter, Rollie Fingers, and Sal Bando stopped shaving their upper lips. Finley liked the look so much that he offered three hundred dollars to anyone who grew a mustache before Father's Day.

The entire team including Williams and his coaches had mustaches. Fingers went the extra mile and grew a handlebar mustache. He still has it to this day.

The Athletics won the AL West by five and a half games over the White Sox and played the Tigers for the AL championship. Detroit won the AL East by half a game over the Red Sox, who played one fewer game than the Tigers because of the player strike.

Fair? Probably not, but who cared? The players went out on strike, so the hell with 'em. Play the damn game.

The A's were in Chicago for a series against the White Sox in late June when Finley invited Ron Bergman and me to his office on Michigan Ave. While there, Charlie picked up the phone and told his secretary to "call Bill Bartholomay." He was the Atlanta Braves' owner.

"Bill, this is Charlie. I want to trade you Denny McLain for Orlando Cepeda."

The entire conversation came over loud and clear on Charlie's speakerphone. He didn't tell Bartholomay that he had two writers in his office listening to every word of the potential trade. The deal was completed, and "Cha Cha," as Cepeda was called, joined the Athletics a few days later.

But he played only a week or so of games, was injured, and missed most of the remainder of the season. The A's moved on without him and didn't miss a beat.

They captured the AL West title and won the first game of the '72 playoffs against Detroit. The Tigers won the second game, a game that included a bat-throwing incident involving shortstop Campy Campaneris, who took exception to an inside-at-the-knees pitch Lerrin LaGrow threw. Campaneris retaliated by throwing his bat at the pitcher. Not a good idea.

Campy was suspended from the remainder of the series by league president Joe Cronin, a Hall of Fame player. Finley, a hall of fame pain in the ass, was not happy. On the night prior to game three in Detroit, the Bay Area scribes were having a quiet, happy time at L. C. Lindell's, a popular watering hole near Tiger Stadium.

Around 1:00 a.m., Tom Corwin, the Athletics' PR director, walked into the sports bar, found the Bay Area writers, and informed us that Finley wanted to meet us at the team's hotel. On the edge of being half in the bag by now, the writers departed the sports bar and walked back to the hotel, where Finley, manager Dick Williams, and Campy were in the lobby. It was now close to 1:30 a.m.

"Follow me," Finley bellowed. "We're going to see Cronin."

He was the Pied Piper, and we were the followers, piling into the elevator. Up, up, up we went. Finally, the elevator stopped, we all got out, and Finley led us to Joe Cronin's room. Charlie knocked three times. The door finally opened, and there stood this Hall of Fame former player, dressed in white cotton one-piece pajamas with a red and white nightcap. He looked absolutely hilarious. Finley berated Cronin for suspending Campy and demanded that his shortstop be reinstated.

Cronin slammed the door shut, and those in the area not named Finley or Campaneris subdued our laughter the best we could. I almost peed my pants, it was so funny, and the whole charade made for a great story in the next day's *San Jose Mercury-News*. Because of the three-hour time difference, I was able to get a story to the paper before the final deadline.

Even without Campy, the Athletics beat the Tigers and advanced to the World Series against the Big Red Machine in Cincinnati—without Reggie Jackson, who tore his hamstring while scoring the winning run in the decisive game.

It was a game started by Blue Moon Odom and finished by Vida Blue. The long holdout at the beginning of the season took something out of Vida, and he was nowhere near the same pitcher that he had been in '71. Williams used Vida out of the bullpen during the postseason. Odom complained of sickness during the final game against the Tigers and had to come out of the game.

Blue came in, held the Tigers at bay, and was the winning pitcher. As he entered the clubhouse after the game, Vida saw Odom, put both of his hands on his neck (signifying that Odom could not handle the pressure), and all hell broke loose. The two teammates had to be separated before they killed each other.

The team flight to Cincinnati was lively. The players celebrated. The media watched. It was a good time for all.

The Reds were such overwhelming favorites that the so-called experts predicted a Reds sweep. Would the Athletics even score a run?

Catcher Gene Tenace, who had caught Vida Blue's no-hitter the previous season, hit home runs in his first two at bats. As a reward, the Athletics player, known as "Steamboat" by friends and family, received a death threat from an armed fan attending the game. The threat would be kept quiet for the remainder of the Series, which the Athletics won in seven games—six of them decided by one run.

On the flight back to Oakland, the charter airplane seemed to rock and roll with the celebrating players and their families. I had a good time exchanging hugs and kisses with Yolanda McGwire, one of the few Athletics front office employees.

The traveling contingent to Cincinnati did not include the Athletics "ball girls" who had been with the team in Detroit. Charlie decided to send Debbi Sivyer and Mary Barry back to Oakland.

The ball girls were another of Charlie's brainstorms. Debbi was stationed down the left-field line, and Mary was down the right-field line. Their tenures as ball girls ended after the '72 season.

Debbi eventually married a Stanford student who majored in marketing, and she became Mrs. Debbi Fields—yes, *that* Mrs. Fields. They developed her grandmother's cookie recipes into a gold mine.

Mary, meanwhile, married Bob Moore, a tight end for the Stanford Indians and later for the Oakland Raiders. Bob was another multiple-sport star from Klamath Falls, Oregon, and had played on the American Legion team I covered in 1964.

After writing a season wrap story for the *Mercury-News* the day after the World Series clincher, I was back on the desk editing other writers' stories and writing headlines. Real life had returned.

Around the middle of December, I received an envelope in the mail. It was a letter from Josten's. The letter disclosed that I would be receiving a World Series ring and they needed the size of my ring finger.

Needless to say, I got that ring size back to Josten's before anyone (i.e., Charles Oscar Finley) changed their minds. For all the bad things he did, I always appreciated Finley's gesture on this one. It was his idea to give Ron Bergman (his number-one enemy among the media) and me World Series rings. (I received three World Series rings in all—one for me, one for my dad, and one for my son. The last time writers received rings was in 1975.)

Chapter 3

1973: Back to Back, with a Caveat

For the first time since the franchise was located in Philadelphia, the Athletics opened spring training as the reigning World Series champions.

The roster included several new players, including catcher Ray Fosse, acquired in an off-season trade with the Indians. Dave Duncan and George Hendrick went to Cleveland in the deal.

Another significant roster change occurred at first base. Left-handed hitting Mike Epstein, who hit twenty-six home runs in 1972, was dealt to the Rangers. The move was twofold: the Athletics wanted to move World Series hero Gene Tenace to first base and give Fosse most of the work at catcher. Also, Epstein had been benched for game seven of the World Series in '72 because he was in an A-Rod-like playoff slump, and he had not taken the sit-down well. That did not sit well with manager Dick Williams.

Camp opened with high expectations for back-to-back World Series championships, something that had not happened in the major leagues since the Yankees managed it in 1961 and 1962.

Team owner Charlie Finley made his annual trip to Mesa, Arizona, and brought along some jewelry. He made a hands-on presentation of the World Series rings at HoHoKam Stadium and told the players, "If you win the World Series again this season, I'll give you rings that make this one look like a high-school ring."

Finley also brought to spring training several dozen of his new orange-colored baseballs. He had been trying since 1970 to get MLB to accept this brainstorm of his. Commissioner Bowie Kuhn relented in the spring of '73 and allowed Finley to use the balls in one Cactus League game.

The orange baseballs were used in the A's 11–5 loss to the Indians in Mesa. The pitchers complained that the balls were too slick and they couldn't grip them properly when throwing breaking pitches. It was the first and, I believe, the only time the orange baseballs were used in a professional baseball game at any level. Charlie was really disappointed and ended up giving many of them away as souvenirs. I had one of them but have no clue where it is now.

The Athletics bolted to a 33–13 record and never looked back, winning the AL West for the third consecutive season. Oakland had three twenty-game winners—Catfish Hunter, Ken Holtzman, and Vida Blue—and the American League's MVP in Reggie Jackson.

But the infighting that had reared its head in Detroit during the AL Championship Series in '72 returned. Reggie was going through a midseason slump, and third base coach Irv Noren commented on the star's struggles. Those comments were not at all derogatory, but Reggie took them that way anyway.

Noren "thinks he was Mickey Mantle or something," Reggie said. "He couldn't carry Mantle's jock." Out of respect for Irv, I did not report Jackson's comments. I considered the source and moved on.

Jackson regained his batting stroke, slugged thirty-two home runs, and drove in 117 runs. Captain Sal Bando, the glue that held this team together, played in all 162 games and led the team in hits with 174. Center fielder Billy North was the leading base-stealer with fifty-nine, and Rollie Fingers had twenty-two saves.

Deron Johnson became the team's first designated hitter and contributed nineteen home runs, sixty-one RBIs, and one of the most memorable moments of the season—he tried to walk out of a hotel room without first opening the door. He had one too many at a players-only team party. Ron Bergman, Glenn Schwarz, and I also were invited and were in the room at the time. Seeing DJ on his back, I volunteered my services to help get him back on his feet and out the door. This time the door was open.

The '73 Athletics played hard and partied hard. They were very good at both. One night on Chicago's Rush Street, Bergie and I ventured into a popular watering hole early in the morning and ran into several of the A's' players including Catfish Hunter and Mike Hegan. They were playing pool, and Hegan had only to make the eight ball—and describe the shot—to win the game. He called a double bank into a particular corner pocket, and Catfish drawled, "If you make that shot, drop your pants and I'll kiss your ass."

Hegan made the double-bank shot into the corner pocket he called, dropped his drawers, and received a smooch on the booty. The bar bouncer told everyone in the group including Bergie and me to leave the premises.

Every season, Finley invited the team to his farm in LaPorte, Indiana, for a summer picnic. Charlie spared no expense, flying in fresh lobster from Maine to go along with lots of beef. There was enough food to feed an army, and Charlie always had his family on hand—sons, daughters, grandsons, granddaughters.

Pitching coach Bill Posedel, one of the finest (and strongest) people I have ever met, enjoyed his scotch. He introduced me to the beverage on one of my first cross-country flights with the team. Fortunately, I didn't much like the taste of the stuff and needed only a matter of days to recover.

On this particular trip to Finley's farm, the festivities were nearing an end, and the players were boarding the bus taking them back to Chicago. Posedel leaned over to pick up one of Charlie's granddaughters, grabbed ahold, stood up, and kept right on going, landing on his back on the lawn. The redheaded granddaughter ended up straddling Posedel's chest. The players cheered the landing.

Posedel, by the way, was the person most responsible for Rollie Fingers becoming a relief pitcher. Actually, Rollie played a role in that too: he was a lousy starting pitcher.

At one point during the season, Finley persuaded manager Dick Williams to use second base as a revolving position. Dick Green would start most games at second and be replaced by a pinch hitter when it was his time to bat—usually eighth.

Another player, like Ted Kubiak, would take over on defense until it was his turn to bat, and the process would continue throughout the game. Six players shared the position during the season: Dick Green, Rich McKinney, Dal Maxvill, Kubiak, Tenace, and Manny Trillo.

Thankfully, the experiment was short-lived.

The summer of '73 came and went, Secretariat won horse racing's Triple Crown, and the Athletics surged into the postseason, facing the Orioles in the best-of-five AL Championship Series. The Birds won the opener, 6–0, behind Jim Palmer before the Athletics retaliated with two nail-biting wins: 6–3 in game two, scoring two runs in the eighth and one in the ninth, and an eleven-inning, 2–1 thriller at the Oakland Coliseum. The Orioles overcame a four-run deficit against Blue to tie the series at 2–2, and the Athletics advanced to their second straight Fall Classic when Hunter blanked the Orioles, 3–0, in game five.

It would be an unforgettable World Series against the NL (National League) champion Mets—unforgettable for all the wrong reasons.

The Athletics won the Series opener, 2–1, at the Oakland Coliseum. Game two became one of the most memorable in Fall Classic history. The legendary Willie Mays, playing center field, misplayed a routine fly ball in the ninth inning, enabling the Athletics to score two runs and send the game into extra innings.

Reserve infielder Mike Andrews was used as a pinch hitter late in the game and remained in the game at second base. He committed two errors in the twelfth inning, paving the way for the Mets to score four runs and win, 10–7.

As the team prepared for the cross-country flight to New York, the reporters sensed that something was going on behind closed doors at the Coliseum. They wondered why Andrews was nowhere to be found in the clubhouse. Our stories would have to be written without quotes from him.

My colleague John Lindblom was not traveling on the team charter like I was, so he was able to hang around the clubhouse longer. He learned that Finley had forced Andrews to sign an affidavit that his shoulder was injured and that he therefore could not continue to play. I wondered why a sore shoulder could have anything to do with ground balls going through Andrews's legs.

Finley's plan was to replace Andrews on the roster with Trillo, who was not on the team's roster prior to the September 1 deadline and therefore ineligible—barring an injury. All hell broke loose when word got out that Andrews was being removed from the roster.

The Athletics players responded by taping number seventeen (Andrews's number) on their sleeves during the off-day workout at Shea Stadium. Commissioner Bowie Kuhn got wind of the pressure Finley had put on Andrews to sign the bogus affidavit and ordered the A's owner to reinstate Andrews to the active roster. Mike was used as a pinch hitter in the eighth inning of game four and received a rousing ovation from the 54,817 fans. Finley fumed and, after the game, ordered manager Dick Williams not to use Andrews again.

Williams was so angry that he told the team before game five in New York that, win or lose, he was going to resign, although he had one year remaining on his contract. Dick O'Connor of the *Palo Alto Times* broke the story. There were the usual denials, but Williams was good to his word. After the team returned to Oakland and finished off the Mets in seven games, Dick announced his resignation.

Shortly thereafter, the Yankees' first-year owner, George Steinbrenner, and Williams agreed on a contract for Dick to manage the Bronx Bombers in 1974. Finley wished him well. However, A's executive John Claiborne convinced Finley to seek compensation from the Yankees. After all, Williams was still under contract to manage the Athletics.

Finley changed his mind about wishing Williams well and asked the Yankees to trade prospects Otto Velez and Scott McGregor to Oakland for Williams. The Yankees would not do that, and Charlie subsequently sued Williams in federal court to prevent him from managing in New York. Finley won his case, and Williams never managed the Yankees.

The ongoing compensation impasse kept me busy that offseason. The winter meetings were being held in Houston that year, and I attended them for the *Mercury-News*. A couple of days before the meetings, I called Finley at his office in Chicago to get an update on the Williams situation.

I asked him five or six questions. He had the same answer for every one of them: "None of your fucking business."

I thanked him for his time, hung up, and had to find another angle for the story.

Ron Bergman and I were in the hotel lobby in Houston when Finley arrived midmorning. After Charlie checked in, we asked him if he had time for an interview. He gave us his room number and told us to meet him at two o'clock that afternoon.

A few minutes before two, Bergman and I met in the lobby and took an elevator to the floor Finley was staying on. We went to the room number he had given us. Bergman knocked, but there was no answer. We went to an adjoining room, and Bergie knocked again.

A grumbling voice emerged from the other side of the door: "Who is it?"

Bergie answered, "Bergman and Street." The voice on the other side of the door instructed us to go to the adjoining room. We waited for a few minutes. The door opened, and there was Charlie, wearing a raincoat and black high-top shoes. It was weird. He chastised us for waking him up at this hour (two in the afternoon), saying he was a "sick man and on medication." He then took a couple of steps toward us. Bergie stepped back, but I didn't.

All of a sudden, Finley lunged out with his right hand and gouged my face with his fingernails. He noticed that I was bleeding and invited us into his room. He went into another room and emerged a few minutes later with a cold washcloth. Charlie patted my wounds and apologized profusely.

He also gave us a forty-five-minute interview.

As Bergie and I started to leave, Finley asked me to stick around for a few minutes. He asked me not to say or write anything about his actions, saying that he had been told by the commissioner that, in light of the Andrews fiasco, if he did anything more to embarrass baseball, he would be suspended. I wasn't sure if assaulting a sportswriter would be considered an offense worthy of a suspension.

I rejoined Bergie, who had remained in the hallway, and returned to the hotel lobby. As we got off, Chicago sportswriter Dave Nightengale saw my scarred nose and said, "Did Finley do that to you?"

I never answered, went to my room, and wrote my story.

The '73 season included the debut of eleven-year-old Stanley Burrell.

Burrell sold stray baseballs and danced with a boom box at the players' parking lot at the Oakland Coliseum to earn money for games. Finley, a rare visitor to Oakland, saw the kid doing splits and hired him as a clubhouse assistant and batboy, giving him a baseball cap with the letters VP on the front.

Burrell served as a batboy with the team from 1973 to 1980, earning, among other things, a nickname: "Hammer." He was a spitting image of Hank Aaron, and Reggie Jackson, who had a way with nicknames, gave the dancing dude a good one.

Burrell also was known among the players as "Pipeline."

After serving Charlie well for seven years, performing such duties as giving his boss a play-by-play of the Athletics home games and supposedly spying on players in the clubhouse, Stanley Kirk Burrell became known as M. C. Hammer.

He made, and lost, a fortune.

Chapter 4

1974: A Two-Ring Circus

Owner Charles O. Finley was so busy trying to find a replacement for departed manager Dick Williams that he had little time to fiddle with the roster. He eventually hired Alvin Dark as the manager. Basically the entire team from the 1973 World Series returned.

Just as he had done the previous spring, Finley came to Mesa, Arizona, in March to present the World Series rings to the players. The reactions to seeing the ring for the first time were different this time.

"My high-school ring looked better than this," Catfish Hunter said in his distinctive Southern drawl. He was referring to the promise Finley had made the previous spring when he told the players that if they won the World Series in '73, he would make the '72 ring "look like a high-school ring."

He failed miserably. The '73 ring was a virtual copy of the '72 ring, and the majority of them did not have any diamond—a World Series ring first. Finley was still angry about the Mike Andrews debacle and used the rings to show his displeasure.

The players were not happy, but that didn't show up on the field as much as it did in the clubhouse. Hunter won a career-high twenty-four games, and the Athletics won ninety games to capture their fourth straight AL West title.

To say everyone got along would not be accurate.

On June 5, outfielders Billy North and Reggie Jackson engaged in a clubhouse fight at Detroit's Tiger Stadium. Jackson injured his shoulder, and catcher Ray Fosse, attempting to separate the combatants, suffered a crushed disk in his neck, costing him three months on the disabled list.

Meanwhile, Finley, who signed Allan Lewis as a designated runner in 1967 and kept him through the '73 season, decided he wanted Olympic sprinter Herb Washington. The world-class speedster had not played baseball since high school, but Charlie made him the team's new designated runner.

Washington was just as fast as Lewis. He appeared in ninety-two games that season, stole twenty-nine times, and was caught stealing sixteen times.

Unfortunately, I missed most of Washington's stolen bases and getting caught stealing, because the *Mercury-News* decided not to cover the team on the road that season. I was crushed. The Athletics had won back-to-back World Series championships, and the *Mercury-News,* one of the most profitable newspapers in the Bay Area, decided that it cost too much money to cover the team full-time.

The *Oakland Tribune* and *San Francisco Chronicle,* which had not traveled with the team until the '74 season, got all the stories.

I spent the summer of '74 covering A's and Giants home games and courting my future wife—Debra Noren, the daughter of Athletics third-base coach Irv Noren. We met at a spring training game in Scottsdale, Arizona, and hit it off pretty well. I learned later that Irv had said, "Be nice to him; he has a car."

We went out to dinner quite often that spring and also to the greyhound races. Debby was an art history student at Cal Poly Pomona, and when the Athletics went on the road, I would sometimes travel to Arcadia, California, where she lived with her parents, for a visit.

The romance blossomed, and we were engaged in July. When the players found out about the engagement, they razzed their third-base coach about his daughter marrying a sportswriter. "It could be worse," Irv said. "It could be Bergman!"

The A's coasted to a fifth straight AL West title, finishing five games ahead of the Rangers, and played the Orioles in the AL Championship Series.

During a workout prior to the playoff opener, team captain Sal Bando was asked about the team's chances of advancing to a third consecutive World Series. Sal said the team's only worry was overcoming Alvin Dark, the manager who had replaced Williams. "He couldn't manage a meat market!" Bando declared.

Oakland dispatched the Orioles in four games, losing the opener and then winning three straight by scores of 5–0, 1–0, and 2–1.

It was on to Los Angeles for the World Series against the NL champion Dodgers.

The workout had not even started when I walked into the visiting clubhouse at Dodger Stadium. Bergman arrived minutes later, and both of us sensed something was not quite right.

During the workout, we learned through the grapevine that pitchers Blue Moon Odom and Rollie Fingers had gotten into a fistfight in the trainer's room over a family-related comment from Blue Moon. Neither pitcher was injured. Anyone with any knowledge of the team knew the A's were game-ready for the Dodgers.

After splitting the first two games in LA, the Athletics won three straight for their third straight Fall Classic title, the first time a team had won that many in a row since the Yankees in the late 1940s and early 1950s.

Herb Washington, the designated runner, was used as a pinch runner with right-hander Mike Marshall on the mound in game one. Washington beat the pickoff throw the first three times. The fourth pickoff toss nailed him. Washington was released on May 5, 1975, ending his MLB career.

Meanwhile, prior to game one, Chicago sportswriter Jerome Holtzman wrote a story saying Catfish Hunter would attempt to become a free agent after the season, citing a breach of contract. Finley had not paid an insurance company $50,000 as stipulated by Hunter's contract.

No one in MLB history had been declared a free agent, and I was among those that didn't pay much attention to the story. We should have taken notice.

Hunter was declared a free agent in December, and although Finley offered to pay his star pitcher the $50,000, he ignored it and eventually signed a multimillion-dollar deal with the Yankees.

It was the beginning of the end for the Mustache Gang. For me, it was the beginning of married life.

On November 16, 1974, in front of family and friends in Arcadia, California, James Franklin Street and Debra Jo Noren became husband and wife, to live happily ever after, et cetera, et cetera. Athletics infielder Ted Kubiak was the best man, and little Robbie Street, one of my two nephews, was the ring bearer.

Chapter 5

1975–1978: The 49ers Years

W hen it came to love and potential matrimonial bliss, the third time was a charm. Previous serious relationships never had panned out for one reason or another. While stationed at the Presidio of San Francisco for the final six months of my US Army commitment, I met and fell head over heels for Beverly Louie, a china doll who worked in the public information office.

After a six-month romance, the thought of marriage entered my mind for the first time. But it dissipated when I realized the difficulties a mixed-race marriage would create. It was not as acceptable in society back then as it is now. So I ended the relationship soon after taking the part-time job at the *Mercury-News*.

Several months later, I met Donna Sporleder, a very attractive and nice person, through Chet Wood, a co-worker at the *Mercury-News*. Donna was a flight attendant for an international airline based out of Oakland. Our friendship grew stronger as time passed, and her parents, Bert and Betty, (I learned later) were sure that I would become their son-in-law. I thought that was possible—until Donna ended the relationship. Ouch.

I took my '68 Mustang for a long drive to the Monterey Peninsula, slept in the car, and drove back to San Jose the following morning to recover from the rejection.

I decided to devote my energy to my job—covering the Athletics. Then Debra Noren came along and stole my heart, big time. The fact

I no longer was traveling with the Athletics didn't seem so bad after our marriage, as we got to spend more time together, working on our relationship and tennis games.

At some point in 1975, the sports editor asked if I would be interested in taking over the 49ers beat. Debby and I talked it over and decided that it would be a good career move, although baseball was still my passion. Road trips in the NFL were two days instead of MLB's two-week journeys, although the *Mercury-News* still was not traveling with either the Giants or Athletics. It was a tough way to cover a team, seeing only half of their games.

The plan was to cover the Giants and Athletics' home games until NFL camps opened in July and then take over the 49ers beat. The team trained in Goleta, California, not far from the University of Santa Barbara campus.

Unlike the Athletics, who became a dynasty in the 1970s, the 49ers were awful. The head coach, Dick Nolan, smoked like a chimney and had a team that got smoked regularly. Steve Spurrier and Norm Snead shared the QB duties. Gene Washington was among the best pass catchers in the NFL, and Delvin Williams was the team's best running back, averaging all of forty-five yards per game.

What I remember most about that team is *San Francisco Chronicle* reporter Jack Smith. He was renowned for his thirst for alcohol and, his favorite beverage was anything that started with an *l* as in *liquor*. Debby and I met Jack for dinner the first night of training camp, and he was bummed about leaving most of his clothes at home. Yep, he had forgotten to pack for the month we would be in Goleta.

Debby and I took him to J.C. Penney's the following morning before practice and helped him purchase some new clothes including a nice plaid sports jacket.

Two nights later, we dined again and asked Jack how he liked the jacket. He said he didn't have it anymore, explaining that he had been in a bar the previous night and some guy had thought so much of the jacket that Jack had taken it off and given it to the guy. Jack was jacketless again.

The 49ers were scheduled to play an exhibition game against the Chargers in Mexico City that fall, but ticket sales were so bad that the game was moved to San Diego at the last minute. Jack walked into the press box about an hour before kickoff somewhat intoxicated. Well, very intoxicated. Actually, he was drunk as a skunk.

He walked (stumbled) to his seat assignment in the front row and tossed his typewriter onto the table. It took one bounce and disappeared, falling some thirty or forty feet into the seats below. It was a heavy typewriter and would have killed anyone unlucky enough to be sitting in the seat that the machine landed on.

Luckily, it was early enough that the seating area was empty. Jack leaned over, got an usher's attention, and asked if he would return the typewriter to the press box. Wish granted. Jack opened the case and found the space bar jammed into the keys, plus other damage, rendering the machine useless.

Jack watched the game, took notes, and dictated a story that was better than the ones the rest of us wrote using operable typewriters. Jack survived the season and eventually took a job at the *Seattle Post-Intelligencer*.

The Jack Smith stories were numerous. One time, while covering the Raiders, he took a cab from the Oakland airport to the team's training camp in Santa Rosa, California. Jack had no money, so head coach John Madden picked up the eighty-dollar cab fare.

The 49ers went 5–9 in '75 and finished second to the Los Angeles Rams in the NFL West. Nolan was fired after the season, and former 49ers player Monte Clark was hired as the head coach. His prior coaching experience included an extended stint as head coach Don Shula's offensive line coach with the Miami Dolphins, and Monte had been on the staff in 1972 when the Dolphins went undefeated and won the Super Bowl.

Monte was huge in stature with a heart of gold, a welcome dose of fresh air following the Nolan regime. Preseason training camp was moved from Goleta to San Jose State University, a ten-minute drive from our house.

The exhibition season included a trip to Honolulu to play the Chargers. As the charter airplane approached the islands, a flight attendant got on the PA and went through a list of places to visit while in Honolulu. Most of them were restaurants and bars.

After she finished, Monte took the phone and said, "Forget everything you just heard. We are here to play football!"

The writers took good notes on the flight attendant's suggestions.

It was a really bad game, 6–3, I recall. Niners placekicker Steve Mike-Mayer won it with a late-game field goal.

Steve was the younger brother of Nick, the placekicker for the Atlanta Falcons. They shared the Atlanta-Fulton County Stadium turf later that season and combined to miss three of their four field goal attempts. Pundits called them the "Miss-a-Miler" brothers.

The 49ers, led by quarterback Jim Plunkett, won six of their first seven games and were the talk of the Bay Area. They then lost four straight and five of six to fall out of the playoff picture. They finished with an 8–6 record, a slight improvement over the previous season.

During the off-season, Monte invited Debby and me to a Burger King grand opening in San Jose. Monte and Don Shula had entered into a Burger King partnership, and one of the guests at the grand opening was Monte's friend and fellow USC graduate, Orenthal James Simpson, known as OJ.

Prior to the 1977 season, the 49ers were sold to Edward DeBartolo Sr., a wealthy real-estate developer from Youngstown, Ohio. He had made a fortune building shopping malls. He had a son, Eddie Jr., who was nearing his thirty-first birthday. As a present, he gave young Eddie the 49ers.

Eddie, in turn, gave the 49ers faithful a rude awakening. Junior was young and brash and seemingly full of himself. The popular Clark was fired. An old codger named Joe Thomas was hired as general manager. Ken Meyer became the head coach, and the team returned to its losing ways, going 5–9.

Meyer lasted one year. On the day he was fired, I left a phone message at his home in Saratoga, California, a swanky San Jose suburb. As I was writing my story at my desk at the *Mercury-News,* my phone rang. I answered, and Meyer was on the other end.

He obviously had been drinking, as his words were slurred. The conversation was brief: "Jim, this is Ken Meyer returning your phone call. I want you to know that I think you treated me fairly," he said. "On the other hand, I think you were horseshit."

Click. I didn't get a chance to say good-bye.

Thomas pegged Pete McCauley as the next head coach. Pete lasted nine games (one win) and was canned. Next up was Fred O'Connor. He went 1–6 and was fired at the end of the season.

The star running back that season was OJ Simpson, who led the team with 593 yards. But the highlight of the season for me was playing OJ in tennis a couple of times during preseason camp at San Jose State. Who won escapes me, but the thing that stood out the most was the size of his head. It was huge, larger than any noggin' I had ever seen.

Thomas did not like the media and vice versa. During a road trip to Washington DC, Thomas was so incensed about an article *San Francisco Examiner* reporter Frank Blackman had written that he confronted the writer on the dance floor at the team's hotel headquarters and took a swing at him. Like most of his coaching hires, Thomas's punch missed badly.

The ultimate highlight that season occurred about two weeks before camp opened at San Jose State—the birth of a bouncing baby boy, Scott James Street, on June 26, 1978. I covered a San Jose Missions baseball game that night and returned home just in time to take Debby to the hospital in Mountain View. Her water broke just as I walked in the door around 11:30 p.m. Scott entered our little world about ten hours later.

The lowlight of that season came on the Mondays following another 49ers loss.

Thomas had a second-floor office at the Redwood City complex and would invite all of the writers covering the team (five of us) to his office. He had copies of each of our game stories and complained about our "negativity."

The more he talked, the more worked up he got. Before he was finished, his baby-blue shirt was drenched with perspiration from his armpits to halfway down his shirt. It was not a pretty sight.

He took the game stories from those twelve losses real hard. I longed for the good old days with the Athletics.

During the off-season, I received a tip that the 49ers were going to hire Bill Walsh as the new head coach. Walsh was the highly successful coach at Stanford and was, I thought, a perfect fit for the Niners job.

I could not get anyone to confirm the tip, but I wrote a story anyway using the words "a reliable source." The next day, Tony Ridder, the *Mercury-News* publisher, came up to me at my desk and congratulated me for breaking the story. He had known about Walsh's impending signing but hadn't been able to say anything.

DeBartolo announced the Walsh signing the following day.

Thomas was ousted as the general manager, and months later, with Walsh in charge of the '78 player draft, the 49ers selected, among others, Joe Montana and Dwight Clark. They went 2–14 that season, but it didn't feel nearly as bad as the 2–14 record the previous season.

One of the highlights of the year occurred after the season, when I visited my older brother Ron in El Cajon. His youngest son, Robbie, asked me to participate in a show-and-tell session at his elementary school, Flying Hills.

I was thrilled to do it. I talked about my job and showed the students my World Series ring. I'm sure his classmates were as thrilled as I was ... and then again, perhaps not. Only Robbie knows for sure.

Chapter 6

1979–1980: Back to Baseball, Thank Goodness

Four years of covering the 49ers seemed like a lifetime. The team was awful, and although Bill Walsh was now the head coach and the passing combination of Joe Montana and Dwight Clark was in place, I accepted an offer to return to baseball as the Giants beat writer.

It was a full-time gig, which meant traveling with the team. Debby and I talked it over at length and decided that it was the best career move for me. The tough part would be the separation between husband, wife, and new baby boy for two weeks at a time during the summer. They accompanied me to spring training in Arizona.

Scott was introduced to his first spring training—first in Casa Grande, Arizona, and then in Scottsdale.

The Giants had some solid talent including former A's Vida Blue and Billy North. Jack Clark, Darrell Evans, and Bill Madlock were excellent hitters and future stars.

Clark was a good hitter, but Jack was not the brightest light in the chandelier.

On a flight from San Francisco to New York, I was riding in the seat behind him and his girlfriend. As the plane approached the Big Apple, Jack turned around and asked, "What's the name of that big building here?"

I said, "The Empire State Building."

"That's it! The Umpire State Building," he said. "Thank you."

I said, "My pleasure."

Joe Altobelli was in his second year as the Giants manager. He would not make it to the end of the season. The Giants got off to a poor start, never recovered, and wound up with ninety-one losses.

Alto was an old-school skipper and extremely proud to be a big-league manager. So proud that when a San Francisco–based young radio reporter addressed him as "Coach" during a pregame media session in Alto's office at Candlestick Park, Joe told the kid to leave the office, get a media guide, and find out what his job title really was.

The red-faced kid walked out of the room.

"I'm a manager," Alto fumed, "not a coach."

Another time, *SF Chronicle* reporter Ira Miller questioned Alto about his use of relievers Randy Moffitt, a right-hander, and Gary Lavelle, a left-hander. Altobelli had been using both, playing the percentages. But one or the other had not been used in this particular game when he normally would have been used.

After the game, Miller asked Alto if the relievers were still considered equals.

"What kind of question is that?" Alto bellowed. "We just won the game. Go shit in your hat."

That was the end of the postgame interview with the manager.

Alto was replaced at midseason by Dave Bristol, who lasted a little more than a year.

The Giants had played an August series in New York and flown cross-country to Los Angeles to begin a three-game series against the Dodgers. It was the same day Yankees catcher Thurman Munson died in a plane crash.

Debby and Scott had flown from San Jose to Los Angeles. She left Scott with his grandparents and drove to downtown LA to meet me at the hotel where the team was staying. She had not told me she was coming, so instead of taking the team bus from the airport to the hotel, I accompanied *Chronicle* reporter Bruce Jenkins, who had decided to rent a car.

We arrived at the hotel several minutes later than the team. Debby was waiting for me in the lobby. She acted a bit fidgety, but it didn't dawn on me that I was in for some big news. At dinner that night, she broke the fabulous news that she was pregnant. Katy Marie Street was born on March 17, 1980, right in the middle of spring training. I rushed home and made it in plenty of time for the birth.

The Giants finished next to last in the NL West that season, but there were no indications of a pending managerial change—not even during the annual winter meetings, which were held in Atlanta that year.

One of the regular events during the meetings is the managers' luncheon. The beat writers get together with their respective managers for some food and chatter about the upcoming season. I sat at the SF Giants table with other Bay Area writers.

Bristol was late. We waited. No Bristol.

Finally, a club official came into the dining room and whispered something to the PR director, and we were told to accompany him to the team's hotel suite. Big news—Bristol had gotten into an argument with the general manager and had been fired on the spot.

Chapter 7

1981: Back to Football

The burden of being a stay-at-home mom with two young children only eighteen months apart in age was becoming increasingly difficult for Debby, so we had another family discussion and decided that the life as a baseball writer was not working out that well. Being away from home two weeks or more at a time was just too much of a burden on her.

The Oakland Raiders beat opened that fall, and I requested a move from the Giants to the Raiders. The sports editor, Terry Galvin, agreed to the move, and it was full-speed ahead on my return to the NFL. The 49ers were a poor team most of the time I covered them in the mid-'70s. Furthermore, General Manager Joe Thomas and some of his head coaches were, in my mind, bad people.

But they were saints compared to the Raiders' Al Davis and Al LoCosale—the frick and frack among disgusting human beings. Despicable, awful, horrible, lousy, rotten—just about any derogatory adjective fit them perfectly.

Upon arriving in Santa Rosa for the start of training camp, Davis sidled up to me on the practice-field sideline and muttered, "Did you stab someone in the back to get this?"

"This would be the *last* beat I would want to get by stabbing someone in the back," I responded.

Covering the Raiders must have been like covering the KGB in the Soviet Union during the height of the Cold War. LoCosale, who apparently never visited a dentist, was Davis's henchman, grumpy, mean, angry, and utterly useless to anyone not named Al Davis.

Tom Flores was the head coach and a really nice person—the antithesis of his boss. He was quiet by nature and pleasant to interview. Jim Plunkett, whom I had covered with the 49ers, shared the Raiders QB position with Marc Wilson.

The Raiders posted a 7–9 record that season, failing to make the playoffs. "Commitment to Excellence," Davis's favorite slogan, was tarnished. The team moved to Los Angeles, becoming the Los Angeles Raiders in 1982. I was not unhappy about the move. Good-bye, Raiders!

The Raiders' farewell season coincided with the beginning of the 49ers' glory years.

After the 49ers got off to a sluggish start, losing two of their first three games, *Mercury-News* colleague Mike Antonucci famously (or infamously) wrote off the season, writing that it was the same old tired, losing story that not even a genius like Walsh could fix.

The 49ers won twelve of their final thirteen games that season and won the division championship. I figured crow must be being served regularly at the Antonucci household.

With the Raiders done for the season, I was part of the *Mercury-News* playoff coverage team. A 14–3 playoff victory over the New York Giants set up a 49ers-Cowboys NFC championship game at Candlestick Park.

On the Monday before the game, I planted a seed with the sports editor, Dan Hruby: if the 49ers beat the Cowboys and advanced to the Super Bowl in Detroit, I would accompany former Raiders head coach John Madden on the train to Motown. Madden, who had retired from coaching in 1978 because he hated to fl y and wanted to spend more time with his family, was just beginning his new career as an analyst for the CBS Television network. CBS would televise the Super Bowl.

The sports editor thought it was a good idea, so I made train reservations from Oakland to Detroit—pending a 49ers victory over the Cowboys.

The Cowboys were heavy favorites in the title game, but it came down to the last minute. I had a great view of The Catch from the front row of the football press box at Candlestick Park. Pals Joe Montana and Dwight Clark became household names on that play.

The Catch remains a big part of 49ers history. But people tend to forget that after the catch, the Cowboys drove into 49ers territory and still had time to kick a game-winning field goal. But Lawrence Pillers forced a fumble, Jim Stuckey recovered the loose ball, and the Niners ran out the clock.

I received a one-way train trip to Detroit—with John Madden and another sportswriter, a guy from Dallas who had pitched the same idea to his boss as I had to mine.

Unlike the Texas scribe, I had more baggage than just my suitcase, and it made me just a little apprehensive about the journey.

Four years earlier, in 1977, I was covering the 49ers. The schedule called for the Niners to open the regular season in Pittsburgh against the Steelers, and the following week, the Raiders would play the Steelers in Pittsburgh.

To save travel costs, the *Mercury-News* sports editor decided it would be a great idea to switch beats for a week—I would cover the Raiders the week before the season opener in Oakland, and the Raiders beat writer would cover the 49ers and then stay over in Pittsburgh, waiting for the Raiders' arrival.

Final roster cuts were made during practice on Monday. The Raiders, coached by Madden, were the only NFL team that did not release information on which players they had cut to reach the opening-day player limit. Every team in the NFL knew, but the Raiders refused to give the names to the media.

I had become friends with Jack White, the 49ers' vice-president of player personnel; and, knowing the Raiders' policy of not releasing the names of released players, I made an arrangement to call him at a certain hour on Monday afternoon, and he would give me the names of the Raiders players that had been cut.

I interviewed several players at the Monday workout, made the phone call, and wrote my story for the next day's *Mercury-News*. We were the only paper that had the names, which was a good thing.

The reaction in Oakland was not a good thing for me. I went to practice the day the story appeared and conducted more interviews. At the end of practice, Madden called me aside.

"Where did you get that information?" he asked.

"Can't tell you," I said. "Did I get all the names correct?"

"Where did you get the names?" he said.

"Can't tell you," I responded.

"Well, it seems to me that you can get the information you need from outside, so there is no reason for you to be here."

I was banned from Raiders practices.

Fortunately, I had enough information from previous interviews to write a couple of advances for the upcoming season opener. But I needed at least two more stories.

Thanks to a phone call *Mercury-News* publisher Tony Ridder placed to NFL commissioner Pete Rozelle, the ban was lifted. I was able to cover the Raiders' practice on Friday and the game on Sunday.

Madden cordially answered the questions I had after the game, a Raiders win, and I was thrilled beyond words to drive to Redwood City the next day instead of going back to Oakland.

Madden recalled the incident in the book *One Knee Equals Two Feet* he wrote with Pulitzer Prize–winning writer Dave Anderson of the *New York Times*. He said he probably overreacted and felt bad about it. In retrospect, I should have gone to him after I received the names and asked him for a comment—good or bad.

But I was mostly young and dumb back then.

Our paths did not cross again until the train ride to Detroit. I boarded the train in Oakland, and the first stop was Martinez, where Madden boarded. We exchanged greetings, and I explained my assignment, which was to interview him along the way for a three- or four-part series leading up to the Super Bowl.

He could not have been nicer, and it became one of the most pleasant assignments of my forty-year career. He had done several Miller Lite commercials and commented that he had become better known as a beer pitchman than he ever had as a head football coach.

Amtrak made numerous stops along the way, and a few hours east of Denver, somewhere in Wyoming, there was a so-called whistle stop in a very small town. It was about midnight when the train stopped. Madden invited the other writer and me to get off the train and accompany him to a small bar not far from the train station.

We walked in to a rousing ovation for the coach from the patrons and walked out a few minutes later with thick sandwiches and a six-pack of Miller Lite, all on the house, thank you. The train would not depart until we had returned and boarded.

Turns out this was his regular routine, as he traveled exclusively on trains to his next TV assignment. He later traveled by bus.

With the Raiders moving to Los Angeles, I returned to the 49ers beat in '82. My return to football hit a bit of a snag when, ten years after going through the first player strike of my career—the major-league players struck in 1972—the start of the NFL season was delayed because of a player strike.

This was especially disconcerting for Niners fans, still savoring the Super Bowl victory over the Cincinnati Bengals. The season schedule was sliced to nine games, and the 49ers won only three of those nine games, becoming the fifth team in NFL history to enter a season as the defending Super Bowl champion and miss the playoffs the following season.

The 49ers also became the only team in history to win more than half its road games while losing all its home games. It was an overall lousy season for the reigning NFL champs—and time for me to get back to baseball.

Chapter 8

1983: A Reunion with the A's and Giants

The career boomerang that I had been on for a few years took another turn to baseball when, with a new sports editor in the *Mercury-News* house, I went back to covering the A's—with Debby's blessing. The kids were four and three years old and attending preschool, which made it easier on her than when both were infants.

Scott had become an avid 49ers fan by now, wearing all sorts of Niners gear. Katy was a pistol, cute as one could get and a bit feisty. I credited her feistiness to something that had happened to her in 1981. I had washed and waxed our new burgundy Volvo wagon and parked it in the garage. Debby put Katy in the plastic carrying device to carry her out of the house and place her into the car seat. All of a sudden, I heard a loud scream and went running out to the garage. Debby had placed Katy on the hood of the car. Debby had then gone to open the garage door. The plastic contraption holding Katy had slid off the slick hood, and she had landed facedown on the concrete garage floor.

She ended up with a badly swollen eye, the first shiner of her young life. There apparently was no other damage. A few days later, and the shiner really black and blue, we nevertheless took the kids to downtown San Jose, where President Jimmy Carter was making an appearance.

We were standing next to the rope keeping the crowd back when Carter walked up to us. Katy was in my arms, turned backward. I turned her around to introduce her to the president of the United States.

His eyes got the size of saucers when he saw Katy's black eye! It was a sight I would always remember.

The new sports editor, John Rawlings, came up with a game plan for the baseball season. The *San Jose News* had folded, leaving columnist John Lindblom without a specific job, and Fred Guzman had covered the Giants the previous season. Rawlings assigned another writer to cover the 49ers, and I was included in a three-way coverage team for baseball, which was fine with me. It would mean less travel overall, and I could return to my passion—covering baseball.

Steve Boros, one of the finest people I ever met in the game, was the Athletics manager. Rickey Henderson, the best base-stealer I ever saw, played left field. Henderson, who had swiped an MLB record 130 bases the previous season, pilfered 108 bases in '82, getting caught just nineteen times.

During interviews, he always would refer to himself as "Rickey."

The starting rotation was young, and the team finished a distant fourth in the AL West, twenty-five games behind the White Sox. The season highlight occurred on September 29 at the Oakland Coliseum, where Mike Warren, making his ninth and final start of the season, pitched a no-hitter against the White Sox—Warren's first complete game of the season and of his career.

Across the Bay Bridge, the Giants had a slightly better record but finished fifth in the NL West. It was not a good season for baseball in the Bay Area, but the 49ers returned to their winning ways and advanced to the NFC Championship game, losing to the Washington Redskins.

Frank Robinson was the Giants manager in '83 and for some reason took a liking to me. But he changed my name. I became "James Boulevard," and it was a name that stuck with him for that season and beyond. To this day, whenever our paths cross, he calls me James Boulevard.

Johnnie LeMaster was the shortstop known more for his glove than his bat. In fact, a few years earlier, when I had covered the Giants, his offense had been so bad that the fans had booed him just about every time he came to bat. So, late in the season, he sauntered to the plate, and the name stitched on the back of his jersey was "Boo." The fans loved it. The general manager, Spec Richardson, did not and ordered LeMaster to change back to his real jersey.

At the end of the '83 season, Rawlings called the three baseball writers into his office and informed us that I would be covering the World Series. After the meeting, in a one-on-one meeting, he said he was sending me because "I thought you did the best job during the season."

The Series that season was between the Orioles and Phillies. I loved it, because it meant I could travel to both sites by train. I enjoyed flying, but the comfort of a train was even better.

Memorial Stadium in Baltimore was located in a residential district far from the nearest hotel. Most MLB teams stayed at the Cross Keys Inn, about a thirty-minute cab ride from the stadium. Kit Stier of the *Oakland Tribune* and I decided to share a cab to and from the hotel on the workout day.

A young writer was standing alone outside the hotel lobby door looking somewhat lost. I introduced myself. His name was Bill Plaschke, and he had just been hired by the *Seattle Post-Intelligencer*. His first assignment: cover the World Series. I asked him if he wanted to hitch a ride with Kit and me, and he did. It would become one of the most important gestures of my career.

I covered both the Giants and Athletics during MLB's annual winter meetings in 1983. Late one night, I received a tip that the A's were interested in signing free-agent second baseman Joe Morgan, who had grown up in Oakland and was nearing the end of his Hall of Fame career.

Unable to get in touch with the A's general manager, Sandy Alderson, for a comment—it was almost midnight—I returned to the hotel lobby to look for anyone who might help me out. I saw Tom Reich, Morgan's agent, come out of the hotel bar.

I introduced myself and asked about the Morgan rumor.

"I have been drinking," Reich said, "and I do not comment about my clients when I've been drinking. I also want you to know that I am probably the smartest person you will ever meet in your life."

My story in the next day's *San Jose Mercury-News* said, "Morgan's agent Tom Reich neither confirmed nor denied the rumor."

Morgan signed a one-year contract less than a week later.

As for the "smartest person" comment, I think not. Ken Griffey Sr. was one of Reich's clients in the '70s and '80s, but the agent did such a lackadaisical job for the veteran outfielder that Senior fired him and hired Brian Goldberg, a young attorney from the Queen City. Griffey and Goldberg had met at a class at the University of Cincinnati in 1978 and had become friends.

When the Mariners made Ken Griffey Jr. the number-one selection in the 1987 amateur draft, he was represented by Goldberg, who also started representing Senior before the 1988 season.

So, by not paying more attention to Griffey Sr., Reich missed out on the millions of dollars he could have made as Junior's agent. In my book, that makes Tom Reich one of the dumbest people I have ever met in my life.

Chapter 9

1984: Dark Days Ahead

The '84 season began with the annual trip to spring training in Arizona. Debby and the kids packed their things, and we headed south.

I started out covering the Athletics in Phoenix. I pitched an idea to sports editor John Rawlings to do a story on what a day in spring training is like for a player. I would wear an Athletics uniform, go through an entire workout, and write a story about it.

He liked the idea. Before the Cactus League began, I picked a day to work out at second base, and future Hall of Fame second baseman Joe Morgan was kind enough to be my tutor. I caught a few grounders; I missed a few grounders. The power stroke I didn't have when I played remained nonexistent. But it was a hoot and made for what I thought was a good story.

The regular season started with the three-way coverage team in place.

But sometime in May, I believe, Rawlings called me into his office and informed me that I was being reassigned. I would become the San Jose State beat writer when the football season began.

Stunned beyond words, I finally said, "Why?"

He said, "Because I'm the boss, and I make those decisions. If you don't like it, you can leave."

The *Mercury-News* had been regarded as one of the best newspapers in the Bay Area to work for. Both papers in San Jose, along with the

Pasadena Star-News, were owned by the Ridder family. They cared about their employees, and everyone I knew worked hard to make the *Mercury-News the* paper in the Bay Area. There was little turnover in the sports department. You basically worked until age sixty-five, or whatever, and retired.

I expected to spend my entire career at the *Mercury-News.*

But the Ridder family sold out (in more ways than one) to the Knight Corporation, a media conglomerate headquartered in Miami. The *Philadelphia Inquirer* was among the major newspapers owned by Knight, and Rawlings was an assistant sports editor.

Then he became sports editor of the *Mercury-News.* And all hell broke loose. He ruled by fear. Several longtime sportswriters quit, landing jobs elsewhere. I stayed, never imagining for a second that I would not continue my career covering professional sports.

The beat switch did not sit particularly well. I couldn't understand how I could go from being assigned to cover the World Series in 1983 because I had done a good job to being demoted and assigned a college beat several months later. It was never explained to me the way I thought it should have been explained.

My days as a baseball writer were supposed to end shortly after the All-Star Game, which I had been told I would help cover. The game was being played at Candlestick Park.

Mostly, though, I was working desk shifts five days a week, writing an occasional nonbaseball story. One of them was on Matt Biondi, a world-class swimmer at the University of California-Berkeley. It was a "takeout" story as we in the business called them. I drove up to Berkeley and interviewed Biondi, the Cal swimming coach, and several of Biondi's swim teammates.

While I was obtaining information for the story, I left several phone messages with Biondi's high-school coach. Days passed, the story deadline approached, and I still had not heard from the coach. When I visited Cal, the sports information director gave me several articles written about Biondi including an article that had been published by a national swimming magazine. The story included quotes from his high-school coach.

I used one of them, one I would regret using.

Several days after the story appeared in the *Mercury-News,* Rawlings called me at home and demanded that I come to the office immediately. Naturally, I was concerned though unaware of what I should be concerned about.

He was not happy when I walked into his office.

He asked me about the quote from the high-school swimming coach. Where did I get it? I told him. He got angrier, explaining that he had received a phone call from the author of the swim magazine article and accused me of using the quote without attribution. Rawlings said I should have credited the quote to the magazine.

I did my best to explain that the quote was pretty innocuous, but I apologized. Yes, I should have attributed the quote, but Rawlings didn't let up. He said I had embarrassed him and the *Mercury-News* and therefore was being suspended without pay for two weeks. Furthermore, I would not be covering the All-Star Game in San Francisco. Gulp!

I returned home completely flabbergasted and unsure about my future. I had two young kids, a wife, and a whole lot of trouble lurking on the horizon.

The suspension and dock in pay were removed several days later. As I discovered later, several of my colleagues in the sports department went to Rawlings and told him that they too should be suspended because they often used quotes from other publications for their Sunday notebooks without attribution and it was a widespread practice in the industry.

I was reinstated. From that point forward, virtually all notebooks had a disclaimer at the end: "Information from other writers was used for this report." It would become a nationwide disclaimer.

I returned to work, primarily on the copy desk. A couple of weeks before SJS began football practice, Rawlings said he had scheduled a luncheon with SJS head football coach Claude Gilbert. I was to attend, and the assignment was written on my work schedule.

On the morning of the meeting, I received a phone call at home from assistant sports editor Gary Richards. He told me that the writer scheduled to cover the A's game that night in Oakland had called in sick, and I was assigned to cover it. I asked about the luncheon, and he told me he would talk to Rawlings and get the luncheon postponed until the following day.

I drove to the *Mercury-News* at midafternoon to check out a company car and drive to the game in Oakland. When I walked into the sports department, Rawlings was in his office. I could almost see the smoke coming from his ears. He was angry as hell, and we met behind closed doors. He yelled at me so loudly that I think those in the room were worried about my well-being.

He said I had embarrassed him by being a no-show at lunch. I explained that Richards had called me to change my schedule. I walked out of the office, went to the bulletin board where the schedules were posted, and saw that my schedule had, in fact, been changed. I removed it, took it into Rawlings's office, and showed him.

It didn't matter. "Get out of here and don't come back until I tell you to come back," he yelled.

I didn't cover the A's game that night or any night. I never again covered a baseball game, or any game, for the *Mercury-News*.

A week or so passed and no word from Rawlings. By now, the stress was so far off the chart I could barely make it through a day, let alone a night, wondering what the hell had happened. I maintained daily contact with Dennis Deisenroth, my best friend in the sports department. He told me that Rawlings had called him into his office several days after I left and said, "I know you and Jim are good friends, and I hope that friendship doesn't affect our relationship."

To which Dennis responded, "Our relationship? We don't have a relationship."

My stress level was climbing daily. Dennis suggested that I see his doctor and perhaps get some medical advice. I explained to the doctor what had happened at the paper, and he said that under no circumstances should I go back to work without his permission.

I filed for California worker's compensation. The *Mercury-News* fought it. A worker's comp representative interviewed several sports department employees, and she came to our house interview me. It lasted more than an hour.

The state accepted my claim, and I received all of my back wages. I remained out of work for another two months, receiving full pay for the unscheduled "vacation." Rawlings finally called and said we should talk. I drove to the office for a meeting with Rawlings and the newspaper's managing editor.

We reached an agreement, and I was reinstated. I learned later that a large majority of the sports department employees interviewed in the compensation process backed my version of what had happened, not Rawlings's, whatever his version was.

I spent the remainder of my *Mercury-News* career writing headlines and proofreading other writer's stories.

Meanwhile, the stress I was having caused much damage in my marriage. By the end of 1984, I had a job back, one that I didn't like, and the devastating news that my wife wanted a divorce.

Chapter 10

1985: A Life Turned Upside Down

A new year started with me working on the copy desk at the *Mercury-News,* a marriage in shambles, and living in an apartment with a bedroom that consisted of an army cot and a closet for my clothes. My efforts to reconcile the marriage failed. I recommended marriage counseling. We had two sessions with a marriage counselor, and I begged Debby not to break up our family but efforts to save the marriage failed.

In order for my kids to stay in the house, I continued to make all of the house payments and pay all the house-related bills including the electricity, garbage, water, and phone. I eventually had to give up the apartment because I couldn't afford it and move in with former Buckwood Court neighbors Greg and Brooks Dunivant, who lived about forty-five miles away in Walnut Creek with their son Tyler.

Shortly before the '85 NFL season started, I received a call from George McFadden, the former 49ers public relations director. He asked if I would help launch the *49ers Report,* a weekly publication dedicated entirely to the Niners. It was a full-time job, five days a week, seven hours a day.

The work schedule I had at the *Mercury-News* was from 3:00 p.m. to midnight with an hour for dinner. My hours at the *49ers* Report were 7:00 a.m. to 2:00 p.m., giving me enough time to drive from Redwood City, where the *49ers Report* office was, to the *Mercury-News.*

The company leased a car for me—a Ford Escort—and I drove it from the *Mercury-News* at midnight to Walnut Creek, slept three or four hours (on a good night), got up at 5:30 a.m., and drove to Redwood

City. My social life took a hit, but on my days off, at least I was able to visit my kids and take them to the park or a movie.

Besides helping to put the paper together with my editing skills, I also wrote some stories. I am not sure what the *49ers Report*'s circulation was, but I know it was small, nothing compared with the *Mercury-News.*

At some point during the NFL season, Rawlings called me into his office—again. Now what? He said he had heard I was writing stories for the *49ers Report* and I had to stop writing for them or else leave the *Mercury-News.* I explained that I wasn't writing for the paper in San Jose, so how was I competing?

He didn't buy my reasoning.

For the remainder of the season, and my stint with the *49ers Report,* I used the name Scott Rhodes as my by-line. I never attended another 49ers game or heard another word from Rawlings on the subject. In the meantime, I attempted to get a job at another—*any* other—Bay Area newspaper. No luck.

In October of 1985, I received a phone call from Bill Knight, the sports editor of the *Seattle Post-Intelligencer.* He said two of his writers had recommended me to fill the soon-to-be-open position as the Seattle Mariners beat writer.

The writers were Jack Smith and Bill Plaschke.

Knight (nicknamed "Stormy") arranged to fly me to Seattle for an interview on the Monday before Thanksgiving. He took me to Ray's Boathouse for lunch, and I returned to Seattle that night.

It was several days before I heard from Stormy. Finally, around December 10, he called and offered me the job. I told him I would get back to him the next day, as I wanted to discuss it with my former wife and Ted Kubiak, her husband-to-be. Kubiak, the best man at our wedding, was now living in the Buckwood Court house, although to his credit, he had called me during our separation wanting to know if there was any way that our marriage could be repaired. If not, he wanted to take her out on a date. I gave him a green light.

The three adults met and talked it over, agreeing that it would be best for my career to accept the offer from Seattle. Arrangements would be made for me to visit the kids as often as possible.

I accepted the offer from Seattle.

A few days earlier, Rawlings invited me to lunch at The Plateau 7, one of the premier downtown restaurants in San Jose. As we waited for the food to be delivered, he said that he was aware I had been talking about the Seattle job and wondered, if I received an offer there, if was any chance I would turn it down and remain with the *Mercury-News,* which was what he wanted me to do.

Under the circumstances, I figured it was best to accept the offer from the *Post-Intelligencer* and move on rather than remain at the *Mercury-News* and face an uncertain future.

Before my departure, the sports department employees gave me a going-away party. The desert was a cake. When it was time to cut the cake, columnist Mark Purdy said, "We don't think it would be a good idea for you to take this knife and cut the cake. You might use it on Rawlings!" Everyone except Rawlings laughed.

I walked out of the *Mercury-News* for the last time on December 22, said a tearful good-bye to my kids, and drove north to Dorris, California, to spend Christmas with my parents.

Chapter 11

1986: A Rejuvenated Career in Seattle

B ill and Lisa Plaschke spent the 1985 Christmas holidays with relatives and insisted that I stay in their house on Mercer Island until spring training started or until I found an apartment. The kind gesture was a big help in adjusting to the new life I was beginning.

I went to work at the *Seattle Post-Intelligencer* the first week of January, beginning a thirteen-year stint at the newspaper as the Mariners beat writer. Bill Knight, the sports editor, understood the situation with my kids and allowed me as much time as possible to spend with them, whether it was during the summer, when school was out, or the winter, when I would travel to California to visit them. Debby had married Ted Kubiak, and they moved to Poway, California.

Quality time with Scott and Katy replaced quantity time, and the first time they visited Seattle, in the summer of '86, we took a two-week trip to Canada. The trek included stops in Vancouver, Lake Louise, and Calgary. We returned via Idaho and really had a grand ol' time. Another time, we went to Sunriver, Oregon, riding bikes and horses and winning bingo games at the timeshare I had purchased on one of my trips to Hawaii.

Working for the *Post-Intelligencer* was like working for the *Mercury-News* in the early days of my career. The sports department employees were terrific people and worked hard as a team to put out a good product every day. Stormy would become, without question, the best boss of my newspaper career.

The Mariners were entering their tenth season when I arrived. The franchise, which debuted in 1977, was born out of a lawsuit against Major League Baseball. The Mariners rejoined the American League eight years after the Seattle Pilots were sold to a used car salesman in Milwaukee—Bud Selig—and moved to Suds City. The Pilots existed for only one season.

The competition between newspapers in the Bay Area was strong, but it was nothing compared to the competition between the *Post-Intelligencer* and the *Seattle Times*. I would be butting heads with Bob Finnigan, who became the *Times'* baseball beat writer in 1982. Our paths had crossed often enough in previous years for me to know who he was and for him to know who I was.

He invited me to lunch shortly after I arrived in Seattle. It was a cordial dining experience—a lot of chitchat about the team, the front office, and so on. That was, I would discover later, not the real Finnie.

About three weeks before spring training started in Tempe, Arizona, I rented an apartment in Bellevue. I arranged for the furniture I was to get in the divorce settlement to be shipped to Seattle. I moved in on January 28, 1986—the day the *Challenger* space shuttle exploded.

The Mariners were managed by Chuck Cottier. The hitting coach was Deron Johnson, whom I knew from when I had covered the Oakland Athletics. I called DJ before camp opened to get a feel for what this team was all about. He compared the '86 Mariners to the '71 A's—a team on the verge of something big.

Left-handers Mark Langston and Matt Young and right-hander Mike Moore headed a strong—I thought—starting rotation. First baseman Alvin Davis had been an All-Star and American League Rookie of the Year. Spike Owen was a terrific shortstop, Phil Bradley was an All-Star-caliber left fielder, center field was manned quite capably by Dave Henderson, and Jim Presley stood his ground at the hot corner.

I wrote positive stories throughout spring training. After covering a team that won three consecutive World Series, I figured I knew a good team when I saw one. I jumped on the bandwagon and expected the Mariners, a perennial loser, to move up the AL West ladder, perhaps all the way to the top.

At a luncheon the day before opening night at the Kingdome, Cottier named Owen as the team's captain. Spike had had a terrific college career at the University of Texas. Roger Clemens was one of his teammates.

The season started on a good note. The Mariners were trailing the Angels by two runs in the bottom of the ninth inning, a deficit erased when Presley hit a two-run home run. Presley came to bat again in the bottom of the tenth inning. The bases were loaded, and he unloaded another home run—a grand slam.

The good ship *Mariner* held its own coming out of the gate, winning five of their first eight games. A 4–0 loss to the Athletics in Oakland, however, triggered a six-game losing streak that saw the team score nine runs total. After back-to-back wins to seemingly right the ship, the Mariners lost the final three games of a four-game series against the A's, including a 1–0 shutout in the series finale. An offense everyone expected to be productive was stuck in the mud, striking out at a staggering pace.

Athletics right-hander Rick Langford, on the downside of a stellar career, struck out twelve in his 1–0 victory.

As the Mariners traveled to Boston the following day, April 28, the Red Sox were finishing up a series against the Rangers in Arlington, Texas, that night. Clemens was scheduled to pitch for the Red Sox. The game was rained out, pushing his start back a day—to April 29 against the Mariners at Fenway Park.

Clemens struck out the first three batters he faced, fanned two more in the second and another in the third. I watched major-league history being made. The Mariners struck out twenty times. Every starter struck out at least once. Bradley struck out four times.

The Mariners actually led the game, 1–0, on Gorman Thomas's sixth-inning home run. Moore, though, surrendered three runs in the bottom of the inning, and Seattle lost, 3–1.

That was the beginning of the end for Cottier. The Mariners lost six of their next eight games, falling to 9–19 overall, and Cottier was fired. First-base coach Marty Martinez managed one game before Dick Williams took control of a sinking ship.

Yes, the same Dick Williams I had covered during the Athletics dynasty in the early 1970s. Dick had been a strict disciplinarian when he skippered those great A's teams and brought the same mentality to the Mariners. Free agency was about ten years old by now, the player salaries were much higher, and their reaction to authority was not what it was back in Dick's heyday.

Dave Henderson always played with a smile on his face. That didn't go over well with the new skipper, and Hendu was traded to the Red Sox along with the team captain, Spike Owen, for shortstop Rey Quinones and three other players in August.

The Midas touch Williams had with the Red Sox in 1967 and the A's in the early '70s never materialized in Seattle in '86. The Mariners lost twelve of their final thirteen games of the season to finish with a 67–95 record and fell into last place in the AL West.

Bob Finnigan was not happy.

The *Seattle Times* reporter was unique in several ways. He regularly worked out with the team during early batting practice on road trips. In fact, he had his own Mariners equipment bag filled with his baseball gear. It traveled with the team's other equipment. The bag was unpacked and the contents neatly arranged in the visiting clubhouse locker with the name Finnigan written with a black felt pen on a strip of white adhesive tape. He was one of the guys.

That was something I had never seen before, but I was new in Seattle and kept quiet. In fact, when my son, Scott, went on a road trip with me to Baltimore and New York one year, we shagged some balls during early batting practice at Yankee Stadium. It was a thrill for Scott, because he got to be on the same outfield grass that his grandfather, Irv Noren, had played on in the early 1950s when he played for the Yankees.

Finnie had another trait that surprised me even more than his player-bonding workouts. It was a habit of verbally assaulting any Mariners player who had screwed up on the field. No player, manager, or coach was off-limits to Finnie's abuse in the press box during a game.

Example: the Mariners were playing the Royals in Kansas City on a Sunday afternoon in the summer of '86. They were one run behind and had the tying run on base when Ken Phelps was inserted as a pinch hitter. Phelps struck out.

Finnie did not take it well. "You haven't hit a meaningful home run in your life!" he bellowed.

It must have been the hundredth or so time Finnigan had ripped into a player, and it was getting old. I finally asked, "Why don't you talk to the players to their faces the way you talk about them behind their back?"

"I didn't know you were such good friends," he responded, referring to my relationship with Phelps.

The Finnigan in the press box was the antithesis of the Finnigan in the clubhouse. A tongue lashing upstairs became soothing words downstairs. "Digger," he said to Phelps, "you just missed that pitch, didn't you?"

A few years later in Oakland, Mariners right-hander Brian Holman retired the first twenty-six batters he faced, leaving him one out away from a perfect game. Phelps, now with the A's, came to bat as a pinch hitter and hit the first pitch for a home run.

I turned to Finnigan, who was sitting next to me, and whispered, "Is that a meaningful home run?"

I often wondered what the players would do if they knew Finnigan was berating them every time they screwed up. His verbal attacks lasted for many more years.

The regular season ended, and I moved on to the playoffs, covering the Angels-Red Sox Championship Series and the World Series between the Red Sox and the Mets.

Before the start of the AL Championship Series in Boston, I interviewed Dick Balderson, the first-year general manager. There had been some behind-the-scenes chatter that the Mariners, with a roster dominated by very religious players, were soft and that it had something to do with their strong religious beliefs.

Balderson was candid with his thoughts on the subject. He thought there might be too much religion in the clubhouse and not enough fight on the field. It was a good story for me, as it was selected as the *Post-Intelligencer*'s Sports Story of the Year. I'm not so sure it was as good of a story for him. He took a little heat over his comments, but it blew over and Balderson went to the winter meetings determined to improve the team.

The best he could do during the off-season was trade slugging second baseman Danny Tartabull and pitcher Rick Luecken to the Royals for right-handed pitchers Scott Bankhead and Steve Shields along with outfielder Mike Kingery.

Chapter 12

1987: Hello, Junior!

The American and National Leagues alternated years for getting the number-one selection in the June amateur draft. The Mariners won three more games than the Pirates in '86 but had the worst record in the American League. As luck would have it, it was the American League's turn to draft first in '87.

Owner George Argyros was fed up with the organization drafting high-school players during the early rounds. It usually takes high-school players longer to reach the major leagues than college players, and they cost less to sign. Patience was not one of Argyros's virtues. Actually, I can't think of any virtues he did have right now.

He wanted the Mariners to take right-handed pitcher Mike Harkey, a stud pitcher from Cal State Fullerton, with the first overall selection. The Mariners brass wanted to take Ken Griffey Jr., the son of Cincinnati Reds outfielder Ken Griffey Sr. Junior was a high-school star at football-renowned Moeller.

Roger Jongewaard, the scouting director, had Griffey and Harkey rated the same going into draft day. He bumped Griffey's number up at the last minute and informed Argyros that Griffey would be their choice. Argyros said, "Go ahead, but you had better be right!"

Griffey signed for $60,000 and embarked on a career that would take him all the way to the top—the Hall of Fame in Cooperstown. It was the right decision.

While Griffey was honing his skills in the minors in '87, the Mariners hovered around the .500 mark, finishing the season with a 78–84 record in Williams's first full year as the manager. Second baseman Harold Reynolds, a switch-hitter, led the American League with sixty stolen bases (Rickey Henderson missed much of the season because of an injury). Alvin Davis hit twenty-nine home runs and drove in a hundred runs. Edgar Martinez, a utility player, batted .372 but played in only thirteen games.

Left-hander Mark Langston won nineteen games, one of them a near no-hitter. He lost the no-no with none out in the ninth inning against the Blue Jays. Right-hander Mike Moore lost nineteen games. Lee Guetterman, a soft-throwing lefty, posted an 11–4 record and rotation-leading 3.81 ERA.

Compared to most Mariners seasons, '87 was pretty darn good. They finished three wins shy of the .500 mark, something that had never been done up to that point.

The future looked bright, as three of the starters had won at least eleven games and two others, Moore and Bankhead, had won nine. Would 1988 give Seattle its first winning major-league baseball team?

Early in the '87 season, I decided that I would use some of my United Airlines frequent-flyer miles to begin exploring the world. I had been to Vietnam, Japan, Canada, and Mexico, but I wanted to visit Sydney, Australia. After all, it had been my intended R&R destination while stationed in Vietnam.

The game plan was to go there with a longtime friend, Doc Russo, the Athletics team dentist. But when I mentioned the trip to my son, Scott, he asked if he could go. It took a nanosecond to switch traveling companions.

By the time the baseball season ended, our trip was all set. Our first stop would be New Zealand, and then it was on to Sydney for Christmas and New Year. I had enough United Airlines frequent-flyer miles to get us two business-class seats in a 747.

Our flight departed from LAX at 11:00 p.m. and took us to Honolulu, where we added some passengers and continued on to Auckland, New Zealand. Scott slept. I watched some movies, and we arrived in Auckland the following day.

After spending the night at a hotel in Auckland, I picked up the camper that was to be our home for about a week. I drove around the island, stopping at places like Pahia and Rotorura (the sister city of Klamath Falls, Oregon), and back to Auckland. We went on a fishing excursion and consumed the catch of the day at an onshore barbeque.

I tried to get Scott to count all the sheep we saw, but he laughed out loud and shook his head when we saw what looked to be hundreds of the woolly creatures. The vehicles in New Zealand have the driver's side on the opposite side from US cars. It took a while to master the technique of shifting left-handed.

At the airport, before our departure from Auckland to Sydney, we ran into Virgil Fassio, the *Seattle Post-Intelligencer* publisher. It's a small world.

The flight to Sydney was relatively short, and we got a fantastic view of downtown Sydney as we approached the airport. The bridge, the Sydney Opera House, and the harbor were spectacular. Our first stop was the downtown Marriott, where we spent the first night, Christmas Eve. We had dinner that night atop the Sydney Tower. It was fantastic.

We moved from the Sydney Marriott to the Fraser Hotel, located near the Sydney Harbor, on Christmas Day for a three-day stay. From there we went on a boat ride around the harbor, visited some shops at the Quay, as they called it, and played the tourist role well, including a visit to a kangaroo park.

The Sydney Zoo was on our must-see list. It rained all day we were there, but that didn't stop us from ordering some Streets ice cream. The original plans called for another camper rental. The owner said he had just rebuilt the engine and it was in tip-top shape.

As we drove north toward the Barrier Reef, Scott looked back and noticed smoke coming from the engine. There was a lot of smoke. The engine apparently was leaking oil, causing all kinds of problems. When I filled up with gas, I also had to fill up with oil. We made it as far as Newcastle. I called the owner and told him what was happening, and he suggested we bring it back to Sydney.

I nursed it back, got my money back, and called the Marriott to inquire about a room for the remainder of our stay. They gave us a real good rate, and we ended up having daily excursions to the areas around Sydney including a train trip to the spectacular Blue Mountains.

We also went to Bondi Beach, the most famous beach in Australia. It apparently is more famous for the topless sunbathers than the quality of sand. Scott, all of ten years of age, got an eyeful of the sun worshipers and never said a word.

Our return trip to the US was on another United 747, but this time we had seats in the upper deck of the plane above the first-class section. We had two of the sixteen seats available and two flight attendants. It was, without a doubt, the best flight Scott and I have ever taken together.

Upon my return to Seattle, I received a letter from a high-school student in Ohio. He had been reading my stories in the *Sporting News* and apparently enjoyed them so much that he wanted to become a sportswriter. He asked for some suggestions, and I wrote him back with such tips as "get a good education and write as much as possible."

Jeff Fletcher went to college and landed a job in the newspaper industry—covering the A's and Giants for the *Santa Rosa Press-Democrat*. He was recently hired as the Angels beat writer for the *Orange County Register*.

Our paths have crossed many times, and he always tells me that his parents blame me for Jeff becoming a journalist instead of a doctor or lawyer as they had hoped.

More than 40 years of memories were on
display at the Man Cave in Tucson

Author shows off cache of weapons seized
during a raid in Vietnam

All-Star relief pitcher Huston Street poses
with another "Steeet" in Oakland

The 1973 World Series champion Athletics at
their 40-year reunion in Oakland

Reggie Jackson signed with the Yankees, became Mr. October, and had a candy bar named for him

The two writers that travelled with the team in 1972 received World Series rings

Susumu Fukatsu was a college student/tour guide during two-month stint in Tokyo

Susumu Fukatsu with his wife and daughter during the 2006 World Baseball Classic in Tokyo

Mom and Dad take a brief rest at the Tulelake-
Butte Valley Fair in September, 2013

The author reports to work outside fabulous
PacBell Park in San Francisco

Scott and the author during a golf excursion to Whistler,
British Columbia in the summer of 2008

Mariners fans always had a special place in
their hearts for Ken Griffey Jr.

Chapter 13

1988: It Was Back to Mediocrity

Among the perks I had with the *Post-Intelligencer* was being the Mariners correspondent for the *Sporting News* and *Sports Illustrated*. My job was to send a notes package to each publication each week. I had taken a slight pay cut to move from the *Mercury-News* to the *Post-Intelligencer* but more than made up for that with the freelance work I received with the *Sporting News* and *Sports Illustrated*.

The extra money and the sale of the San Jose house—Debby, Ted, and the kids moved to Poway, California—allowed me to purchase a condominium in Bellevue in 1987, a house in Renton in 1989, and to pay child support for my two kids. I also was able to purchase used cars (Hondas) for both of my kids and, years later, buy another car for Katy when she was attending Cal State Fullerton.

Interest in the Mariners heading into the '88 season was high. They had made solid progress the previous season. The starting rotation was experienced and solid. The offense had been bolstered early in the season by the addition of slugger Steve ("Bye-Bye") Balboni.

But it was bye-bye Dick Williams in the first week of June.

The Mariners split their first eight games of the season, lost to Oakland on April 13, and never reached the .500 mark again. On June 4, a Saturday night in Kansas City, ace left-hander Mark Langston took a 3–2 lead into the bottom of the ninth inning.

Langston retired one batter, but the Royals scored two runs to win the game, and afterward Langston criticized Williams for not making a pitching change earlier in the inning. Williams was livid when he heard about Langston's comments.

The Mariners' record fell to 23–34 the following afternoon with another loss to Kansas City. The team returned to Seattle to start a seven-game home stand. There would be a new manager for the series opener against the Brewers.

Every baseball beat writer and sports columnist attempted to reach Williams by phone. He returned one of them—the one from me.

We arranged to meet at his condo near Pike Place Market in downtown Seattle in the early afternoon. In an exclusive interview with the *Post-Intelligencer* reporter, Williams discussed the firing. I asked him if he thought the Langston reaction had anything to do with the firing.

"I don't know, but I would hope not. Regardless, Mark Langston doesn't have gut one in his body."

Of all the quotes used in the story, that's the one that got the most attention. I don't think, even to this day, that Langston has forgotten those words.

Jim Snyder was named interim manager for the remainder of the season. The Mariners won their first two games with Snyder as the skipper and then lost twelve of their next thirteen to lower periscope and descend into the AL West basement.

General Manager Dick Balderson lost his job midway through the '88 season and was replaced by former Yankees executive Woody Woodward. But before his departure, Balderson traded Ken Phelps to the Yanks for untested outfielder Jay Buhner. It would become one of the best trades in Mariners history.

Even so, the Mariners finished the season with the lowest attendance in the American League. The good vibes heading into the season gave way to more doom and gloom.

On top of that, George Argyros attempted to sell the Mariners and purchase the San Diego Padres. Mark Kreidler, a reporter for the *San Diego Union,* called me to talk about Argyros. He wanted to know what kind of guy he was, what kind of owner the Padres would be getting.

"San Diego is the luckiest city since Beirut," the smart-ass part of me said. I had no idea Mark was going to quote me directly in his story. He did, and Argyros read the quote. He was not happy.

The Mariners took their annual trip to Palm Springs for a Cactus League game against the Angels the following March. Argyros had driven over from Orange County to attend the game—and to see me as well.

Craig Detwiler, the team's traveling secretary, told me George wanted to see me in the visiting clubhouse. George and I had always gotten along well, and I didn't think it was a big deal kind of meeting. He had the story in his hand, read the quote, and gave me the what for.

I tried to explain that I was just being glib and didn't mean anything by it but never said I was misquoted. I don't think George really liked me much for the rest of his tenure as the owner. I felt bad about saying something like that.

But it could have been worse. A few years later, Chuck Armstrong, the team president and the guy George hired to run the organization, was quoted in a book as describing George's ownership method as "Seagull management." What did he mean by that? "He flies in, has lunch, shits on people, and flies out."

Chapter 14

1989: The Kid Reaches the Big Leagues at Nineteen

The thirteenth season in Mariners franchise history started with yet another managerial change. Jim Snyder, who had replaced Dick Williams in June 1988, was not re-signed. It was not surprising, as the Mariners had played as poorly under Snyder as they had under Williams.

I asked General Manager Woody Woodward, who had replaced Dick Balderson midway through the 1988 season, if Jim Lefebvre was on his list of potential managers. He wasn't. I mentioned that I thought Lefebvre, whom I had gotten to know in the '70s when he was a coach with the Giants, would make a good manager. He now was Tony LaRussa's hitting coach with the AL West champion Athletics, and LaRussa had given me a resounding yes when I asked him if he thought Lefebvre was ready to manage a major-league team.

I called Lefebvre at his residence in Scottsdale, Arizona, and told him he might be getting a call from Woody. That call came a couple of days later, and "Frenchy," as he was called, became a Mariners managerial candidate.

Meanwhile, I had driven to Southern California to spend some quality time with my kids. We stayed at Bill and Lisa Plaschke's house in Carlsbad while they were on a trip to Europe. My daily routine included a call to Lefebvre, who kept me abreast of the Mariners managerial hunt. My stories in the *Post-Intelligencer* included any off-the-record information I received from Lefebvre along with any on-the-record information from Woody.

While Bob Finnigan was writing about virtually every ex-manager, or every manager wannabe, I was able to concentrate on Lefebvre, who had reason to think he was a leading candidate. Sure enough, he was selected as the Mariners manager.

The *Post-Intelligencer* got the story first, and it felt especially good, because the competition with Bob Finnigan was intense. He was a terrific reporter, and battling him on a daily basis was stressful, probably for both of us. We had a heated but civil working relationship.

As spring training opened for the '89 season, there was as air of excitement among the Seattle players, and when Lefebvre walked into the clubhouse for spring training in 1989 he was greeted by players wearing "I am a Lefebvre believer" t-shirts.

Ken Griffey Jr. reported to camp as a nineteen-year-old and wasn't expected to earn a spot on the opening-day roster.

But Junior had a superb camp, much better than anyone expected, and accompanied the team to Las Vegas, Nevada, for the final two exhibition games of the spring.

On April 1, 1989, Lefebvre called Junior into the manager's office at Cashman Field 'Vegas and, with a straight face, told Griffey that despite his great camp, and so on, and so forth, he was being sent back to the minor leagues. Junior bit and was visibly disappointed. Lefebvre finally said, "April fools! You're on the team."

The Mariners opened the regular season in Oakland against the Athletics and right-hander Dave Stewart. Junior lined a double to left center in his first at bat. It was Griffey's only hit of the game, and the Mariners lost, 3–2.

The Mariners were outscored 25–6 in a three-game series sweep and then dropped two of the three games they played against the Angels in Anaheim. It was an ugly start to the season.

They returned to Seattle for the home opener against the White Sox with a 1–5 record. There were 33,866 fans on hand at the 52,000-seat Kingdome. Even with the Kid, attendance for home games was poor, and Seattle finished next to last in attendance in the American League.

But Griffey, batting second, made a terrific first impression for the home team. He hit the first pitch he saw from White Sox right-hander Eric King into the seats in left field for his first major-league home run. The Mariners won the game, 6–5.

Junior would play 127 games, hit sixteen home runs, and drive in sixty-one runs as a rookie. Unfortunately, he also would get mad at his girlfriend in his Chicago hotel room, slam his fist against a wall, and suffer a season-ending injury. The mistake cost him any chance of winning the AL Rookie of the Year Award.

But he would capture the Northwest's imagination and have a candy bar named in his honor—the Ken Griffey Jr. Chocolate Bar.

It was a big seller, but Griffey was not a good consumer. He's allergic to chocolate.

Junior became the second player I covered with a candy bar named after him. The first was Reggie Jackson, whose stature and ego increased proportionately during his career.

Reggie once said that if he played for the Yankees, he would have a candy bar named after him.

Sure enough, Reggie signed with the Yankees, became known as Mr. October because of his postseason exploits, and along came the Reggie Bar.

I never ate a Reggie Bar but imagined that the ingredients included chocolate, caramel, some kind of nut—and mustard.

While Junior recuperated from his hand injury in '89, a twelve-game losing streak that started on August 16 ruined any hopes of the Mariners having a winning season for the first time in franchise history.

There were bright spots. Right-handed closer Mike Schooler had a team-leading thirty-three saves; outfielder Jeffrey Leonard had twenty-four home runs and ninety-three RBIs; and Alvin Davis, known as "Mr. Mariner," had twenty-one home runs and ninety-five RBIs. AD's best friend on the team, Mark Langston, eligible for free agency after the season, was traded to the Montreal Expos on July 31—the nonwaiver trade deadline.

Last-minute contract-extension negotiations broke down, and Langston, who wanted to stay in Seattle, left the team and the country, traded to the Montreal Expos. Coming to Seattle were right-handed pitchers Gene Harris and Brian Holman and a lanky left-hander known more for his mullet and wildness than anything else—Randy Johnson, the Big Unit.

The six-foot-ten Johnson, the tallest player in MLB history at the time, moved into the rotation immediately and posted a 7–9 record the rest of the way. He threw hard and was really wild. Randy struck out 104 batters in 113 innings but also walked 71.

The Mariners ended the season with another losing record. As usual, I was assigned to cover the AL playoffs and World Series. That took me back to the Bay Area, where both the Athletics and the Giants won league championships.

The first-ever Battle of the Bay World Series started in Oakland. The powerhouse Athletics won the first two games, prompting longtime *Detroit News* baseball writer Tom Gage to write, "Not even an earthquake can save the Giants."

After a day off, the Series resumed at Candlestick Park.

To save our respective publications some money, Larry LaRue, the Mariners beat writer from the *Tacoma News-Tribune,* and I stayed with Doc Russo in Alameda. We left his house around three o'clock in the afternoon for game three. We crossed over the Oakland viaduct and Bay Bridge between three fifteen and three thirty and drove into the Candlestick Park parking lot. It was early, so finding a good parking spot near the media entrance was a piece of cake.

At around 5:15 p.m., I was at my seat inside the overhanging football press box talking on the phone with Glenn Drosendahl, the *Post-Intelligencer*'s assistant sports editor. All of a sudden, the press box began to shake. Phil Rogers, a writer from Chicago, bolted from his seat on the front row and ran across the top of the table, stepping over computers, notebooks, and anything else in his way. The light standards swayed back and forth; the earth moved.

"We're having an earthquake," I told Drosendahl.

"Can you make it part of your game story?" he asked.

Before I could answer, the phone went dead.

Not quite sure what to do, LaRue, *Post-Intelligencer* sports columnist John Owen, and I waited around to see if the game would be played.

About an hour later, game three was postponed. It was getting dark, and we still had not written our stories. The entire area around Candlestick Park was without electricity.

We piled into my rented car and exited the stadium parking lot, which was jammed with spectators departing as well. We still did not know how extensive the damage was or when we would find a place with electricity. Our information came via the car radio, and it was not good news.

Part of San Francisco was burning, and all of the bridges in the area had been shut down. Having spent fifteen years in the Bay Area, I decided the best route back to Alameda was a roundabout way—go south on Freeway 280 through Daly City, Palo Alto, and San Jose, and then head north on the Nimitz Freeway to Alameda.

As I drove, LaRue and Owen wrote their stories, using the dome light to see their computers. There were no quotes for either of them to use, so they basically wrote about their experience. I had gathered some information from MLB officials at Candlestick Park for a game story.

By the time we found an area with lights, I had driven all the way to Palo Alto. Owen and LaRue had finished their stories. I pulled off the freeway and searched for a phone booth. I'm not even sure if cell phones existed, but none of us had one if they did. While they dictated their stories to their respective papers, I sat in the back of the car and wrote my story.

We finally delivered our stories and drove back to Alameda, arriving well after midnight. Doc Russo was there to meet us. Now he had three houseguests, and we stayed up for another hour or so talking about the wild day. LaRue and I realized that if the quake had hit two hours earlier, we probably would have been on the Bay Bridge, which partially collapsed, or the viaduct that totally collapsed. Thank you again, my guardian angel.

I spent the next few days as a news reporter, driving as far south as Santa Cruz for stories. I also took BART into San Francisco for MLB commissioner Fay Vincent's news conferences at the Fairmont Hotel, which still did not have electricity.

I returned to Seattle a few days later to await word on when, or if, the World Series would resume.

The Fall Classic eventually resumed, and the Athletics won the next two games, finishing off a four-game sweep of their Bay Area neighbors.

Chapter 15

1990: The Door Finally Opens for Edgar

Going into the 1990 season, third baseman Edgar Martinez was twenty-seven years old and beginning to wonder if he would ever get a chance to play regularly with the Mariners. Despite impressive numbers during his minor-league career, he had received nothing but brief stints in the majors the previous three seasons.

Given an opportunity in '90, the Puerto Rico native ran with it. He played in 144 games and batted .302, marking the first of ten seasons of batting at least .300. Gar wasn't fast by any means, but he had a swing that was as sweet as a stick of Hawaiian sugarcane.

Ken Griffey Jr. recovered from his broken hand the previous season and earned his first All-Star Game selection. The Kid excited the fans more than any player in franchise history. Junior batted .300, belted twenty-two home runs, and drove in eighty runs. He also won the first of his ten consecutive Gold Gloves, signed a lucrative deal with Nike, and became a household name in homes around the world.

The smile was genuine. The swing was smooth and powerful. Junior became the most popular professional athlete in Seattle. He purchased his first house, located less than a mile from my home in Renton. When Scott and Katy came up for a visit that summer, he invited us to his house, which was filled with more video games than furniture. The kids were thrilled to get to spend some time with the Kid. I passed on the video games.

Scott and Katy returned to San Diego with some good stories to tell their friends.

The Mariners hovered around the .500 mark most of the season, but a pair of four-game losing streaks during a fourteen-game stretch assured yet another losing season—the fourteenth in franchise history.

There were some great moments along the way. Randy Johnson went into his June 2 start against the visiting Tigers with a 3–3 record. The game was on a Saturday night, and because the *Post-Intelligencer* did not have a Sunday paper, I stayed home.

Bad move. The Big Unit pitched the first no-hitter in franchise history. The final batter, Mike Heath, swung at a pitch over his head for the gem-ending out. Randy raised his arms in exultation, and catcher Scott Bradley jumped into his teammate's arms. Johnson struck out eight and walked six—par for the course for him.

The crowd at the Kingdome that night was slightly more than 20,000. Seattle was still a football town. New owner Jeff Smulyan sensed that Major League Baseball and Seattle were not a good fit.

A media mogul from Indianapolis, Smulyan had purchased the franchise from George Argyros in 1989. Argyros had bought the team in 1981 for $13.1 million and had sold it to Smulyan and Michael Browning, a real estate developer, for $60 million, plus another $10 million for collusion damages the owners had to pay the players' association.

Argyros called the agreement "good for baseball, good for Seattle, and good for the Mariners." It was especially good for him, as he turned a nice profit. The former owner and new owners all agreed that the team would remain in Seattle and play at the Kingdome.

"Let me say it again and again," Smulyan said. "Seattle, the Mariners are your team."

Well …

Smulyan and the club president, Gary Kaseff, had great ideas and wanted to make the Mariners successful in Seattle. Unfortunately, the money needed to pull it off was lacking. Attendance remained subpar, the local radio and TV contract was among the worst in the American League, and local businesses did not jump on the Mariners' financial bandwagon.

Despite a contest to come up with a new mascot—the Mariner Moose was born—public support was lacking. Even those with deep pockets were reluctant to support the perennial losers.

During his first trip to Toronto with the team, Smulyan noticed a huge video screen in center field at the plush new SkyDome. It was flashing an ad from Seattle-based Microsoft. That was a slap in the face to the new owner, who didn't understand why a Seattle-based company was spending more advertising money in Canada than it was in its own back yard.

On the field, Jeffrey Leonard became a positive influence on Griffey, sort of a father figure, you might say … until his real father arrived.

On August 19, the Mariners signed outfielder Ken Griffey Sr., who had been released by the Reds. Leonard sensed that he would be getting even less playing time, and I sensed his bad mood. I arranged for an interview with him during the first road trip in September.

He explained that if he reached a certain number of plate appearances, his contract would roll over and he would be signed for the following season. He said the organization wanted to make sure he didn't reach that number.

He also insisted that the story not be published until the team returned home from a two-city road trip that ended in Anaheim against the Angels.

Unfortunately for me, *Tacoma News-Tribune* beat writer Larry LaRue had talked to Leonard's agent. Much of what Hack Man told me his agent told LaRue. There were, however, no restrictions as to when the *Tacoma* story could be published.

LaRue's story appeared on the morning of the series opener against the Angels. I decided that I had to run my story the following day. Jeffrey was not a happy camper and gave me some big-league nasty looks in the clubhouse prior to the second game of the series.

Meanwhile, the game began, and the Griffeys, Senior and Junior, smacked back-to-back home runs off right-hander Kirk McCaskill, the first time in MLB history a father-son tandem hit consecutive home runs.

The Mariners lost the game, but the Griffey sluggers were surrounded by the media. Leonard, who did not play that night, began yelling at me from across the room. He finally calmed down, the interview with the Griffeys ended, and I went over to Hack Man's locker to explain why my story appeared earlier than planned.

He was not in a listening mood.

"If I ever see you in a dark alley," he said, "I'll kill you."

"I never go into dark alleys," I responded.

Leonard finished the season with the Mariners, but he didn't get enough at bats to receive an additional year and retired.

I still stayed away from dark alleys.

Chapter 16

1991: Hooray! A Winning Season at Last

K en Griffey Jr. was becoming one of the biggest stars in major-league baseball, and the Mariners were showing signs of becoming a pretty darn good team. Junior was flanked to his left by right fielder Jay Buhner, a power-armed, power-hitting bundle of energy.

The corner infield positions were filled more than adequately with sure-handed Pete O'Brien at first base and Edgar Martinez at third. The double-play combination of shortstop Omar Vizquel and second baseman Harold Reynolds was among the best in the business. Alvin Davis, known as "Mr. Mariner," did most of the designated hitter duties.

One of the reserve infielders was Jeff Schaefer, who became one my best friends on the team. You want funny? Schaef was an absolute hoot. You want a battler? Schaef never just watched an on-field confrontation. He made sure he got right in the middle of it.

The Mariners were in Kansas City and had just promoted infielder Dave Cochrane. He showed up at the park, and the Royals' team photographer went to the Mariners clubhouse and asked for Cochrane. They needed a picture to put on the video screen if Cochrane made an appearance in any of the games during the series.

The photographer asked Schaefer, "Are you Cochrane?"

"Yes, I am," Jeff answered.

A few minutes later, Schaefer was getting his picture taken, wearing large horn-rimmed glasses and the goofiest smile you can imagine. Cochrane entered the game as a pinch hitter, and the picture flashed on the huge screen in left field. Everyone in the visiting dugout and Seattle section of the Royals Stadium press box busted out laughing.

The real Dave Cochrane had his picture taken the following day. It was not the last time Schaefer pulled a fast one.

He returned to the Mariners the following season, signing a one-year contract that included a games-played incentive clause. The regular season ended against the White Sox, and Schaef needed one more game appearance to reach fifty-five and receive a five-thousand-dollar bonus.

While the Mariners took their between-inning infield drills before the top of the ninth inning, Schaefer grabbed his glove and sprinted to shortstop. He told Omar Vizquel that he was being inserted into the game. Vizquel departed, and the game ended with Schaefer fielding a grounder and throwing out the runner at first base.

He later said it was the easiest five thousand dollars he ever made. General Manager Woody Woodward was not pleased. My friend never played another game for the Mariners. It was fun while it lasted.

One thing Jeff and I had in common was that we both were dating Canadian women at the time. On an unrelated note, Jeff's step-dad was a big-time lawyer in New Jersey and did a lot of work for, well, thugs. On one of the Mariners' trips to New York, Scott went with me. Schaefer invited us to his Jersey neighborhood for a round of golf and dinner. It was a great off day.

The '91 Mariners were streaky. They lost their first six games—here we go again—but won eight straight followed by a five-game skid. A 12–1 record from May 3 to May 18 put them eight games over .500. Another cold spell, a seven-game losing streak from May 21 to May 28, left the team one game above the break-even mark.

Five consecutive wins in mid-August put the Mariners an unheard-of ten games over .500, a high-water mark that quickly went south during an eight-losses-in-nine-games skid in early September. The record hovered around the .500 mark through most of the month, climbing on the plus side on September 29 when Randy Johnson outpitched Charlie Hough, 2–1, improving Seattle's record to 78–77.

A 4–3 victory against the Rangers at Arlington Stadium on October 2 was the Mariners' eighty-first of the season. Catcher Dave Valle and designated hitter Alvin Davis were in tears when the media were allowed into the clubhouse. They were tears of joy. Valle, who had joined the Mariners in 1984, went two for three and drove in two runs. Davis, who also debuted in '84, had the best zero for four of his career.

For the first time in franchise history, the Mariners would not have a losing season. They won two more games and finished with an 83–79 record. The Mariners finished fifth in the seven-team AL West, but they had taken a major step.

Griffey batted .327, matched the twenty-two home runs he hit in 1990, and drove in a hundred runs for the first time. He finished ninth in the MVP vote. Jay Buhner led the team with twenty-seven home runs, and Edgar Martinez batted .327. Four starters won at least eleven games, including a team-high thirteen by Johnson and Brian Holman. Bill Swift and Mike Jackson each excelled out of the bullpen.

And what did Jim Lefebvre get for managing the Mariners to their first winning season? He was fired.

Chapter 17

1992: The Good, the Bad, and the Ugly

After giving manager Jim Lefebvre a pink slip at the end of the 1991 season, the Mariners quickly signed longtime minor-league manager Bill Plummer. He was a popular choice among the players, many of whom had played for him at Triple-A Calgary.

Plummer finished the '91 season as the Mariners' third-base coach, replacing Bob Didier, who became the bullpen coach after a string of missteps—such as giving signs on his own during a game. As you could imagine, that did not go over well with Lefebvre.

To make matters worse for Didier, he got on General Manager Woody Woodward's bad side when the team was playing a game in Kansas City. Woodward, who was with the team and sitting behind the visiting dugout, kept hearing a thump, thump, thump.

The noise was coming from the visiting bullpen in left field—the players were having their own game, hitting a beach ball over and over again. It might not have been so bad if the team hadn't been on a losing streak at the time.

Before Plummer moved into the manager's office, the wheels had been put in motion for the Mariners to end their seventeen-year marriage with Seattle. Attendance continued to rank near the bottom of the American League, and efforts to build a new, outdoor stadium near the Kingdome were failing miserably. The plan was to put the team up for sale as required by the lease agreement the Mariners had signed with King County years earlier, figuring that no one with local ties would step up. Smulyan was prepared to move the franchise to Tampa-St. Petersburg, Florida.

The team would have held spring training in Homestead, Florida, in the spring of '93. I learned later that ownership was concerned that Lefebvre would spill the beans and the planned move would be nipped in the bud. Plummer was their ideal one-and-done manager.

A group of Seattle businessmen, including Puget Power executive John Ellis, went to great lengths to find a local buyer who would keep the team in Seattle. Finally, as the deadline approached, Washington Senator Slade Gorton called in some political chips and persuaded Hiroshi Yamauchi, the founder of Japan-based Nintendo, to provide the funds needed for the $100 million purchase.

Several MLB owners voiced their disapproval of Japanese ownership. But it was worked out, and the Mariners stayed put. On July 1, Ellis became chairman of the Baseball Club of Seattle. But money alone, even Japanese dough, was no guarantee that the Mariners would live happily ever after in Seattle.

More than six months earlier, at the winter meetings in Louisville, Woodward had worked out a trade with the San Francisco Giants. He sent pitchers Bill Swift, Mike Jackson, *and* Dave Burba to the NL club for outfielder Kevin Mitchell.

Cincinnati Reds manager Lou Piniella had nothing but praise for Mitchell, saying the slugger was the only hitter in the National League that he would seriously consider giving an intentional walk with the bases loaded. Mitchell was only three years removed from leading the league in home runs (forty-seven) and RBIs (125). Imagine him at the friendly confines (for hitters) of the Kingdome.

The best-laid plans sometimes go awry. Mitchell was injury prone, played in just ninety-nine games, hit nine home runs, and drove in sixty-seven runs. Meanwhile, in San Francisco, Swift, Jackson, and Burba had solid seasons and, up to that point, it became the worst trade Woody made as the Mariners general manager. It didn't help that Mitchell had a bad habit—filling his stomach in the late afternoon, going to the ballpark, and vomiting on purpose. One of those upchucks was so violent that Mitchell strained an oblique muscle and missed almost a week's worth of games.

The departure of Swift and Jackson gutted Plummer's bullpen. He wore a path from the dugout to the pitcher's mound, and on several occasions, he looked into the seating area behind the third-base dugout and shrugged his shoulders. He was communicating the message "What can I do?" to his girlfriend.

I was happy for Plummer when he got the job. Our paths had first crossed in 1965, when I played for the COS baseball team and he was the star catcher at Shasta College in Redding. Plummer was the best player in the league, and soon after our teams split a double-header in Redding (we won the second game, 21–7), he signed a contract with the St. Louis Cardinals as an undrafted free agent.

Meanwhile, Ken Griffey Jr. had another solid season, batting .308 with twenty-five home runs and 103 RBIs. He was selected as the All-Star Game's most valuable player, joining his dad as a Midsummer Classic MVP. Junior's sidekick in right field, Jay Buhner, smacked a team-leading twenty-seven home runs, and third baseman Edgar Martinez had a breakout season, batting .343 and becoming the first player in Mariners history to win a batting championship.

Scoring runs at the hitter-friendly Kingdome was easy. Stopping other teams from scoring runs was practically impossible. Closer Mike Schooler tied a MLB single-season record by surrendering four grand-slam home runs. "I guess I am the epitome of grandslamness," he said after number four.

Randy Johnson led the league in strikeouts (241), including an eighteen-strikeout game against the Rangers. Left-hander Dave Fleming was the most reliable starter, leading the team in wins (seventeen) and innings pitched (228 1/3). Plummer had such little confidence in his bullpen, for good reason, that he wore out Fleming's left arm. The twenty-two-year-old had tossed 17 2/3 innings the previous year, his rookie season, and by the age of twenty-five, Fleming was out of baseball.

By the end of the '92 season, Plummer was out of a job with the Mariners. It was one and done. Seattle, an eighty-three-win team in '91, was a ninety-eight-loss team in '92. Home attendance, which reached an all-time high of 2.1 million in '91, fell to 1.6 million the following season, the twelfth lowest in the American League.

Chapter 18

1993: Lou Piniella to the Rescue

My assignment for the *Post-Intelligencer* during the baseball off-season was to cover the University of Washington women's basketball team. The head coach, Chris Gobrecht, was one of the most successful coaches in her profession. The Huskies were perennial Pac-10 championship contenders. One of her assistants was Sunny Smallwood.

I covered a Huskies home game on November 6, 1992, and returned to the office around 11:00 p.m., after I had written and sent my story to the newspaper. I checked for phone messages, and there was one. It was from an extremely reliable source telling me that the Mariners had reached an agreement with Lou Piniella to manage the team and a press conference would be held either the following Monday or Tuesday.

I told my editor in charge at the paper and wrote a quick story, perhaps eight or nine paragraphs, announcing that Piniella would be the Mariners' next manager. It made the final edition of the morning *Post-Intelligencer*—too late for the *Seattle Times* to react—and was right on the money.

Several news outlets in the Seattle area picked up the story the following morning. Without a Sunday newspaper, I could not write a follow-up story until Sunday for Monday's paper. That gave the *Times* one entire day to confirm, deny, or ignore the story. They ignored it. Bob Finnigan wrote a story for the Sunday *Times* saying that Doug Rader would be the next candidate to be interviewed for the job.

The Mariners called a news conference on Monday, November 9, to announce the hiring of Louis Victor Piniella to a three-year contract.

It was the most satisfying scoop in my seven years with the *Post-Intelligencer*. Finnigan told me later that he also knew of the Piniella hiring and called his office, but they refused to use the information.

Yeah, right.

Finnigan thought he was the king of the beat and hated to get beat on a story. He would never acknowledge it when he did.

The Mariners hit a jackpot with Piniella. He had a terrific track record as a player and manager with the Yankees and Reds, guiding the Reds to the World Series championship in 1990—a four-game sweep over the Athletics. He was a winner and knew how to make other players winners.

Seattle had a couple of things going against it when they approached Piniella: he lived in Tampa, Florida, and the great Northwest was about as far away as he could get from home and still be in the US. The other drawback was that the Mariners had had just one winning season in franchise history.

But the Mariners also had Woody Woodward as the general manager. He and Piniella had worked together with the Yankees and were great friends. It was because of that friendship that Lou consented to a trip to Seattle for a get-acquainted dinner with the owners.

When it appeared that Piniella would just say no, John Ellis suggested that Lou was afraid of the challenge this job entailed. Lou, being the competitor that he was as a player and manager, accepted the offer.

That was the easy part. The hard part was teaching his new players how to win.

Camp opened in Peoria, Arizona, with more fanfare than usual. For one thing, the Mariners had to play all of their Cactus League games on the road, because the stadium at the new complex was not yet built. Secondly, the nucleus of a solid team was in place with the likes of Ken Griffey Jr., Jay Buhner, Edgar Martinez, and Randy Johnson.

The Mariners opened the Cactus League season with ten consecutive losses. Lou was fuming. On the bus trip back to Peoria, he looked out the window, saw a Little League team practicing, and ordered the bus driver to pull over to the side of the road.

"Let's play those guys," Lou said. "Maybe you can beat them."

The Mariners won sixteen of their final twenty exhibition games and set sail on the first season with Sweet Lou in the dugout, ranting, raving, throwing tantrums, and showing the sort of spunk that eventually would rub off on his players. It was Lou's way or the highway!

Soon after accepting the job to manage the Mariners, Piniella convinced Woodward to work out a trade with the Reds for catcher Dan Wilson. A backup in Cincinnati, Wilson had caught Piniella's eye during spring training with the Reds. For whatever reason, all of the pitchers wanted to throw to Wilson.

The Mariners acquired Wilson for second baseman Bret Boone, and eventually he would be inducted into the Mariners Hall of Fame. Oh, yeah. He also had a nickname for me: "Boolie."

Piniella was everything advertised. The fans loved him because of his charisma. When he argued with an umpire, it wasn't short and sweet. His ejections were theatrical. The players laughed and loved it. He was teaching them how to compete and how to win.

Th e defense improved by leaps and bounds. Th e pitching was better, although the bullpen was a work in progress. The season highpoint came early. On April 22 against the Red Sox at the Kingdome, right-hander Chris Bosio walked the first two batters he faced and then retired the next twenty-seven, pitching the second no-hitter in franchise history.

The game ended with shortstop Omar Vizquel making a bare-handed catch of a high chopper and, with his cap flying off his head, making a perfect throw to first base for the game-ending out.

Griffey became the first Mariner to hit at least forty home runs, reaching that number on September 1 and declaring afterward, "I am not a home-run hitter!"

Three weeks later, also at the Kingdome, Dan Howitt hit his first and only career grand slam. It came against legendary right-hander Nolan Ryan. He walked off the mound after that pitch, suffering from a torn ligament, and he never threw another pitch in his Hall of Fame career.

The Mariners also nearly ended Cal Ripken's consecutive games-played streak in '93. That happened on June 6 in Baltimore's new Oriole

Park at Camden Yards. Backup catcher Bill Haselman was hit by a pitch and charged the mound. When order was finally restored, four Mariners were ejected. Ripken, trying to break up the fight, injured his right knee so severely that he didn't think he could play the following game. Luckily for him, the Orioles had a day off, and because of his amazing healing powers, Ripken's streak remained alive.

The Mariners ended the season with an 82–80 record, the second winning season in franchise history. Lou was just getting started.

When he was released, reliever Mike Schooler said, "All this organization cares about is winning."

Meanwhile, up in the press box, Bob Finnigan was ripping the players up one side and down the other when they screwed up and kissing their butts in the clubhouse. He continued his early workout sessions with the team on the road. Where Finnie went, his equipment bag followed.

I was ready to barf but didn't interfere with Finnigan's charade. If only the players knew, but they were just as oblivious to what occurred in the press box as we were oblivious to what occurred in the dugout during games.

The ownership change came at a price for Finnigan. In previous years covering the team, he would have his annual physical at spring training along with the players. The new owners asked, "Why are we paying for his physical?" That was a good question.

From that point on, Finnie had to get his physical exam elsewhere.

Chapter 19

1994: The Mother of All Road Trips

A few years after taking Scott on a trip of a lifetime to New Zealand and Australia, it was time to have a special trip with Katy. So after the 1993 season, we went to Florida for a weeklong vacation.

Our destination was Orlando, where we would tour, among other things, Disney World and Universal Studios and then drive over to the East Coast and check out the Kennedy Space Center at Cape Canaveral.

We spent three days hanging out at Disney World, which included Epcot Center. Among the many rides we took was the Star Wars roller-coaster ride, which was dark, wild, and a lot of fun. But the best thing was the small crowds. There was hardly any wait at all, and we must have gone on the Star Wars ride at least a dozen times.

On our daylong side trip to the Space Center, Katy was amazed by how many armadillos were on the road. Luckily, we didn't run over any of them. From an educational standpoint, the tour of those facilities was superb.

While in Orlando, we took in a couple of Senior League baseball games involving former major leaguers. Their best days were behind them, and the league lasted a year or two before folding.

It was back to work in February 1994 with spring training in Peoria, Arizona. The Padres shifted their spring operations from Yuma to Peoria and, having the choice, elected to use the facilities the Mariners had used the previous year. That was especially good for the media, because the pressroom at the new part of the complex actually had windows! What a concept.

The Peoria Sports Complex also included a new stadium, one that could fit upward of eleven thousand fans. I couldn't help but recall my first camp with the Athletics at HoHoKam Stadium in Mesa. It was a wooden firetrap. Fortunately, the stadium was torn down rather than burning down.

The Peoria stadium was first-class in every way. And it was great not to have to get in a car every day to get to a Cactus League game. The Mariners had some home games! A 21–9 spring record was the best in franchise history by far, and coming off a winning record in '93, hopes were high when the regular season started.

An opening-night crowd of 57,806 was the largest in franchise history. It was a home-sweet-home kind of night as the Mariners defeated the Twins, 9–8, in ten innings, a victory that ended a season-opening five-game losing streak.

The first of those losses occurred at Jacobs Field in Cleveland, the first game played at the new stadium. President Bill Clinton threw out the first pitch and then settled in to watch baseball history nearly be repeated.

Randy Johnson was mowing down the Indians one inning after another. At the end of the seventh inning, he had allowed no hits. A fidgety Bob Feller was sitting in the row in front of me, admiring the way Johnson was pitching, knowing all too well that Johnson was six outs from becoming the second pitcher in MLB history to toss his no-hitter on opening day.

Feller pitched his gem on April 4, 1940, against the White Sox in Chicago.

I don't think he wanted that personal achievement to be matched. I'm sure of it, because he let out a huge sigh in the eighth inning, when with one out and one on, Sandy Alomar singled to right field. The Big Unit uncorked a wild pitch and then a two-run double to Manny Ramirez that tied the game.

The season started with Dan Wilson as the first-string catcher and Bobby Ayala, acquired in the same trade with the Reds, as the closer.

The Mariners had shipped second baseman Bret Boone and starting pitcher Erik Hanson to Cincinnati.

Wilson became a crowd favorite with Mariners fans. Ayala became one of the least popular players in franchise history. The *Seattle Times'* Bob Finnigan's most common response to another Ayala blown save: "You piece of mung!"

Manager Lou Piniella was not off-limits to a Finnigan tirade when he stuck with Ayala in the closer role.

"Big-league manager, my ass," Finnie would say over and over and over. But, as always, his mood was 180 degrees different in the clubhouse or on the field before games.

If Sweet Lou only knew what was being said about him. I came close to telling him a few times but decided against it. Being a tattletale was not my style.

The Mariners' night game against the Royals in Kansas City on June 17, 1994, took a backseat to what was happening in Southern California.

Practically every TV station in the US was filming a bizarre scene—a number of California Highway Patrol cars following a white Ford Bronco. The lone passenger in the car was OJ Simpson, who reportedly had a gun and was contemplating suicide.

OJ was the leading suspect in the murder of his ex-wife, Nicole, and her friend Ron Goldman.

I was in the press box covering the game with one eye and the car chase with the other. Bob Sherwin of the *Seattle Times* and Larry LaRue of the *Tacoma News-Tribune* were doing the same thing.

A Las Vegas–based guy named Hadley (I can't remember his last name), a close friend of Lou Piniella, attended the series and was in the press box during the game sitting in the row behind the writers. He told us he had OJ's cell phone number. We were a little skeptical and asked him to make a call. Hadley dialed the number that he had programmed for OJ on his cell phone.

It rang a few times before there was an answer. "This is OJ. I can't come to the phone right now, but leave your name and number, and I will get back to you."

Hadley left a message ... but as far as I know, he never received a return call from the Juice.

Ken Griffey Jr., while claiming that he was "not a home-run hitter," sure looked like one in '94. On June 17, in the Mariners' sixty-fifth game of the season, Junior hit his league-leading thirtieth home run off Kansas City Royals ace David Cone in a 5–1 Mariners win at Kauffman Stadium.

But wins were hard to come by, and the team limped into the All-Star break with a 37–50 record. Just six days into the second half of the season, things got worse as the Mariners were taking pregame practice for a game against the Orioles at the Kingdome.

All of a sudden, there was a loud noise in the seating area behind the third-base dugout followed seconds later by another noise. Two ceiling tiles had fallen from the roof of the Kingdome and landed in the still-vacant seats. If the tiles had fallen two hours later, it would have caused havoc and probably some injuries.

Unsure how many tiles might fall, the organization decided to cancel the two remaining games of the Orioles series. The remainder of the thirteen-game home stand was rescheduled as road games.

It was good-bye Seattle.

Boston was the first stop. Next up was Detroit, followed by Chicago, California, Kansas City, and Oakland. The mother of all road trips lasted twenty games and covered 10,425 miles, a MLB record previously held by the Astros, who took a prolonged road trip during the 1992 Republican National Convention in Houston.

The road trip (and season) ended on August 12 when the players went on strike, the ninth work stoppage in MLB history. This one didn't bother me nearly as much as the first one in 1972.

The stoppage came just as the Mariners came together as a team. They won nine of their last ten games and crept to within two games of first place in the wacky AL West. Every team went into August with a losing record, and the Mariners were 49-63 when the season suddenly ended. The Mariners looked like the best team in the division.

I expected the season to resume within a couple of weeks or so, and the time off after such a long road trip was welcome. Two weeks passed. Then two more and still there was no settlement. It was nearing the middle of September by now and becoming more obvious that the regular season—and postseason—were on the verge of being canceled.

On September 14, MLB commissioner Bud Selig announced that the season was over and for only the second time in MLB history there would not be a World Series. It had been ninety years since a fall did not include a Fall Classic.

I was among the members of the Baseball Writers' Association of America who voted not to award any of the postseason awards including the Cy Young and Most Valuable Player trophies. But the majority of the writers voted to keep the tradition going. I returned to Seattle and wrote stories on the minor leagues. Katy flew up for a few days, and we took a one-day trip to Bellingham for a story on Baby M's manager, Mike Goff, who had been suspended earlier in the season for mooning an umpire during a game in Medford, Oregon. Goff did not agree with a call made by the home plate umpire and, yes, dropped his drawers. It was that kind of year.

Chapter 20

1995: Refuse to Lose

The premature end to the 1994 season turned into a winter of infrequent talks between owners and players but no action. Both sides dug in their heels like never before, taking the impasse into the following calendar year.

On January 26, President Bill Clinton ordered the players and owners to resume bargaining and reach an agreement by February 6. Unfortunately, the deadline came and went with no resolution of the strike. Just five days earlier, the owners had agreed to revoke the salary cap and return to the old agreement.

Even without a new collective-bargaining agreement with the players, the owners decided to open camps—with replacement players. Most of us thought this was a bad idea, but it's not up to us to tell the owners how to run their businesses. Or ruin their businesses.

The Mariners opened camp in Peoria, Arizona, with a full complement of players, although calling them that is something of a stretch. The replacements included players with some major-league experience, major-league baseball wannabes, and former professional or college players who always had dreamed of playing in the big leagues but never had the talent necessary to reach the highest level of the sport.

The players' association called them all scabs, and they never were accepted by the genuine major-league players. Mariners minor-league outfielder Charles Gipson crossed the mythical picket line, and although he eventually reached the major leagues and played in 373 games—331 with the Mariners—he never paid union dues and does not receive a pension.

Among the most memorable stories that spring concerned Dave Graybill, a Glendale, Arizona, fireman. On the morning before he was scheduled to pitch in a Cactus League game, Graybill, on duty with the fire department, helped rescue badly burned eighteen-month-old twins from a house fire.

Hours later, at Peoria Stadium, he was the winning pitcher in the Mariners' victory over the Cubs.

"I had the worst day of my life in one career," said Graybill, a member of the US 1984 Olympic team, "and then had one of the best days in my other career."

His other career was short-lived.

As far as Manager Lou Piniella and his coaches were concerned, these were among the worst days of their careers, but they had to bite their collective tongues. The position players were smaller, slower, and not nearly as powerful as the players they were replacing. The pitchers didn't throw as hard, didn't have the same quality of breaking pitches, and couldn't command many of their pitches.

But everyone seemed to have a good appetite.

At one point in camp, when it became apparent that the players' weights were rising faster than their batting averages, Piniella ordered a cutback in food intake. Lunches no longer would be an all-you-can-eat buffet. Players were limited to soup and half a sandwich, plus a beverage.

Mariners CEO John Ellis headed a contingent of club executives to Peoria to watch the replacement players in action. Before the first game he attended, Ellis complained to the writers that we were writing too many negative stories and that was hurting regular-season ticket sales. The game plan was to open the season with replacement players.

"So you want us to write lies?" I said. "The quality of players here is not at the major-league level. In many cases, they are not even the minor-league level. I can't say anything good about them other than they seem like nice people."

The strike ended when future Supreme Court justice Sonia Sotomayor issued a preliminary injunction against the owners on March

31. On Sunday, April 2, 1995, the day before the season was scheduled to start, the 232-day strike was finally over. Judge Sotomayor's decision received support from a panel of the Court of Appeals for the Second Circuit, which denied the owners' request to stay the ruling.

The real spring training started on April 3. Teams had three weeks to prepare for the regular season, which was reduced to 144 games from the usual 162. It was the longest spring training of my life—from mid-February to late April.

Fans all over the MLB landscape were angry with the players and displayed their displeasure by staying away from games. The Mariners drew just 34,656 to their home opener against the Tigers, more than 23,000 fewer than the previous season.

After winning three of the four-game series against the Tigers at home and sweeping the Rangers in three straight on the road, the Mariners were off and running with six wins in seven games.

They ended May with a 19–13 record—and without Ken Griffey Jr.

I had taken a few days off before Memorial Day and was on a camping trip with my girlfriend at a lake east of Seattle. On our return trip to Renton on Sunday morning, I stopped at a grocery store to pick up a newspaper, the *Seattle Times*.

The headline: "Griffey Shatters Wrist."

Griffey broke his right wrist in the seventh inning while making a circus catch against the wall at the Kingdome, robbing the Orioles' Kevin Bass of extra bases. A crowd of 15,256 held its collective breath as Junior walked off the field, holding his badly injured wrist. It was a game I didn't mind missing, because it would have been a horrible story to write.

Griffey already had established himself as a superstar and clearly the best player I had ever watched. He could run, hit, hit with power, throw you out with his arm, and beat you with his legs and knowledge.

Oh, he was a pain in the rear at times. I can't count the number of times he demanded to be traded. He had writers scrambling all over the place looking for Woody Woodward after making another demand.

"Oh, I was just kidding, you guys," he would say.

But when Griffey talked, people listened, and the writers wrote.

I recall one time when the Mariners were scheduled to play an exhibition game against a minor-league team in Zebulon, North Carolina, on what was scheduled to be a travel day. Several players complained about it, but their gripes were barely noticed. But when Griffey voiced his disapproval, it became national news.

Junior had that kind of power. And he wielded it often.

When right fielder Jay Buhner became eligible for free agency and was being pursued by the Orioles, Griffey said that if the Mariners didn't resign his best friend on the team and running mate in the outfield, he would leave the organization when his current contract expired. Buhner received a hefty, and deserved, long-term contract from Seattle.

It was Buhner who rallied the troops after Griffey's horrendous injury. He emerged as the team leader, and the team responded, treading water well enough to stay near the .500 mark during Junior's absence.

But the California Angels were far ahead in the standings, leading the Mariners by thirteen games on August 12. However, major-league baseball added a wildcard playoff berth before the '95 season, and that figured to be the Mariners' only path into the postseason.

But Buhner pointed to the AL West race, conceding nothing to the Angels. He convinced many of his teammates to go for the division title, and something unbelievable materialized the final six weeks of the season, a finishing kick that was emotional and exciting. It captured the imagination of every baseball fan that heard the late, great Dave Niehaus describe one unlikely victory after another: "My, oh, my!"

The mother of all comebacks came after the Angels lost shortstop Gary DiSarcina to injury. The team went into a nosedive. The Mariners, simultaneously, caught fire. They won sixteen of the nineteen games between September 7 and September 29, many of them come-from-behind thrillers. A Refuse to Lose sign was spotted at the Kingdome, and the slogan became the team's rallying cry. Just as I was thinking this summer would be just like all others I had experienced since taking over the beat in 1986—meaningless Septembers—a city came to life and loved baseball as much as I did.

It was a wild ride for everyone. Griffey came back and hit a game-winning home run off Yankees right-hander John Wetteland in late

August. Vince Coleman won a game with a grand slam, the only one of his career. Role players seldom written about during the first four months of the season became headliners in September.

Norm Charlton, one of Lou Piniella's Nasty Boys with the Reds in 1990, was signed at midseason and notched ten of his fourteen saves in September. Crowds at the Kingdome during the final eight-game home stand topped 46,000 five times, twice going over 50,000, something that hadn't happened all season.

While all this Refuse to Lose madness was going on inside the Kingdome, Washington residents were set to vote on a measure to build an open-air baseball-only stadium. Club officials were confident the pennant race would sway the vote to the positive side. But the measure barely lost—the biggest loss of the season for the Mariners franchise.

While *baseball* might have been a nasty word in many major-league cities in '95, it was a beautiful word in Seattle, always known as a football town. Among local teams, the Mariners were no better than the third most popular.

One unsubstantiated story I heard said it all. A fan parked his car in the Kingdome parking lot one afternoon, put two Mariners game tickets on the dashboard, came back two hours later, and found four tickets on the dashboard.

But that all changed in '95.

The Mariners not only caught the Angels but took a two-game lead with two games remaining. However, after winning the first two games of a four-game series against the Rangers to clinch a tie for the division title, the Mariners suffered back-to-back losses in Texas. The Angels completed a four-game sweep of the Athletics (A's manager Tony LaRussa benched star outfielder Rickey Henderson for all four games), and the AL West ended in a flat-footed tie.

The Mariners returned to Seattle for a one-game playoff against the Angels. The winner would advance to play the Yankees in the best-of-five AL division series. The loser would go home. A coin flip held in September determined that the Mariners-Angels playoff game would be played at the Kingdome.

As fate would have it, two pitchers involved in the 1989 Seattle-Montreal trade were front and center: Randy Johnson against Mark Langston, the two best pitchers in Mariners history.

My flight from Dallas arrived in Seattle in the late morning, time for me to drive directly to the Kingdome. I also had to make flight plans for New York for later that night, just in case the Mariners won. It was a red-eye, although I was already red-eyed from the wild weekend in Texas and the September to remember.

The Mariners won the playoff game. The season continued.

Champagne flowed throughout the home clubhouse, something that had never happened in Seattle. It was a wild scene as Griffey, Johnson, Buhner, Edgar, Tino, Wilson, Charlton, and Blowers acted like kids. They had combined their immense talent into the franchise's first AL West championship.

Next stop: the Big Apple.

There's nothing quite like a postseason game at Yankee Stadium. I grew up listening and watching World Series games, usually against my beloved Dodgers. Except for 1955, the Yankees always won. I was among those who called the Bronx Bombers the Damn Yankees.

Early in my career, I covered some games at the original Yankee Stadium with the white façade completely around the roof and many steel beams on the second deck holding the roof in place. There were two large headstones on the grass in center field far, far away from home plate. No human, it seemed to me, could hit a ball that far in the air.

The '95 playoffs were played at the refurbished Yankee Stadium, where more than 50,000 fans attended. With Randy Johnson unavailable, the Mariners lost the series opener. The second game went into extra innings until, in the fifteenth inning, Jim Leyritz hit a game-winning home run for the Yankees.

The game ended at 1:30 a.m. ET, giving us about one and a half hours to meet our midnight deadline in Seattle. As we waited near the visiting clubhouse entrance, the Mariners dejectedly came through the tunnel leading to the dugout, turned left toward the throng of media waiting to interview them, and turned right into the visiting clubhouse.

Tim Belcher, the losing pitcher, didn't turn right. He came toward the media, standing behind a painted white line.

He angrily lunged at a cameraman, disrupting the filming segment. Order was quickly restored. The angry pitcher turned around and entered the clubhouse.

We entered the clubhouse a few minutes later, interviewed the manager and players, and returned to the press box to write our stories. The *Post-Intelligencer* contingent of columnist Art Thiel, former sports editor and national writer Bill Knight, and I finally filed our stories at about 3:30 a.m. in New York.

Little did I know that the next time I covered a game at Yankee Stadium, that white line would be moved back about fifteen feet. It became known as the Belcher Line.

With our work completed, I called a limo service (cabs would not go to the Bronx after midnight) for a ride to the LaGuardia Airport Marriott, arriving at about 4:30 a.m. We all had rooms, but our flight left at about 8 a.m. There wasn't much use in getting any sleep, so we asked the hotel clerk if there was a place nearby where we could get a beverage. He pointed us in the direction of a pub, where Frank and Ginger were standing behind the counter.

We introduced ourselves, ordered beer, and proceeded to get into some heavy-duty conversation. Stormy made a comment to Ginger that he probably shouldn't have made, and Frank told the story of how he had whacked a guy because of something the victim had said to Ginger. A good lawyer had come to Frank's rescue, using self-defense as his alibi. It had worked. We gulped downed the brew and headed back to the hotel. To my chagrin, I learned upon getting to the room that I had left my sports jacket in the back of the limo (which was a limo in name only) that transported us to the Marriott. I usually can't sleep on a plane, but I slept like a baby on the return trip to Seattle from New York, having worked something like fifteen consecutive days. The series resumed at the Kingdome in front of 54,000-plus fans including my son, Scott.

Now seventeen years old and a sports nut like his father, Scott had asked me if he could come up from Southern California if the Mariners reached the playoffs. I covered the off-day workout and then drove to the airport to meet him.

The next three days were the best in franchise history. Back-to-back-to-back wins over the Yankees, including a game-five extra-inning thriller that ended when Edgar Martinez hit "The Double," driving in Joey Cora from third and Ken Griffey Jr. from first for a one-run victory. The noise inside the Kingdome was deafening. The place actually shook.

Thank goodness the ceiling tiles stayed put.

Scott returned home with some fantastic memories, and I continued to cover baseball well into October. When players talk about adrenaline, I know exactly what they are talking about. The adrenaline flow during those two weeks kept me going. It definitely wasn't sleep.

The Mariners went on to lose the best-of-seven AL Championship Series to the Cleveland Indians in six games. The most poignant scene in the AL Championship Series finale was rookie Alex Rodriguez consoling a sobbing Joey Cora in the Mariners dugout.

On the day after the AL Championship Series, I was in the *Post-Intelligencer* office writing my season wrap story when sports editor Glenn Drosendahl came up and commended me for the job I had done. About the same time, the *Seattle Times* gave my chief competitor, Bob Finnigan, a nice bonus and a raise. I received a "Nice job." Priceless.

Chapter 21

1996: Another Year of Change

The First Interstate Bank branch in Factoria, Washington, the closest all-service bank to the apartment I rented in Bellevue prior to the 1986 season, was where I opened a few accounts. It also was where I met a teller named Elaine.

During one of our earliest meetings, we started talking about my occupation. I told her I covered the Mariners for the *Post-Intelligencer,* and she commented that she was friends with Alvin Davis, the Mariners first baseman.

I checked it out. Alvin said he did know Elaine and commented that she was a "really nice lady." We chatted during my visits to the bank, and the relationship was totally platonic for several months, during which time she told me she was married (unhappily) and had a son.

I had purchased a condo in Bellevue, and Bill Knight, the sports editor at the *Post-Intelligencer,* was going through a divorce. We worked out a deal where he would become my roommate. This arrangement lasted several months. While on a road trip, I received a piece of mail from Elaine. I asked Stormy to open it up and read it, which he did.

The card was very flattering to me and definitely caught my attention. A few weeks later, Stormy moved out and Elaine moved in. It would be one of the worst decisions of my life. For one thing, she was still married. For another, I had no intentions of getting married again and did not have the same feelings for Elaine that I had for Debby when we were courting. But I discovered a physical love and jumped in with both feet.

Elaine and I agreed that any future marriage was out of the question. Neither of us wanted that kind of commitment. It was imperative for me to be free to spend as much time as possible with my kids over Christmas holidays, summer vacations, whatever. The live-in arrangement lasted eight years, during which time I purchased a house in the Olympus neighborhood where Bill Knight and his new wife, Dorothy, lived.

On a Sunday morning, Elaine and I decided to take a drive to Issaquah and check out the Klahanie housing development, which was relatively new at the time. We saw a worker at one of the houses and chatted for a few minutes. Then we drove back to the condo in Bellevue and, with her son Peter asleep in the back, decided to stop by and see Stormy and Dorothy at their house in Olympus.

After we explained where we had been, Bill told us about a house that was for sale in the neighborhood. We chatted with Stormy and Dorothy for a while and decided to check out the house. We rang the doorbell, and a man answered—the same man we had seen hours earlier in Issaquah.

It turned out he worked for Buchan Homes and had built this house himself as an investment and it was for sale—for $160,000. The price was a bit high, I thought, but after selling another piece of property I had as an investment and renting out the condo, it was feasible to buy the house in Olympus. I qualified for a solo loan (without any financial assistance from Elaine), and we moved into the two-story house in 1989.

Seven years later, Elaine asked, "When are we going to get married?"

I answered, "When the cows come home."

During a visit to my parents' home during the summer of '95, we were staying at the Golden Eagle Motel (the only one in town) when, early in the morning, we were awakened by a cattle drive going past the motel.

"The cows are home!" she exclaimed.

I figured it must be an omen—or a bad dream.

It wasn't a dream. I decided to propose and invited my kids to spend Christmas with us in Seattle that year. With Scott and Katy, along with Elaine's son, Peter, in attendance, I presented a ring to Elaine—hidden in a ceramic cow. She accepted, and we were married in Steamboat Springs, Colorado, in June 1996.

I asked for a divorce about three months after our first anniversary. In my mind, the person I had married was not the same person I had lived with for such a long time. I knew I had to cut the cord and get out of this mess I had put myself in.

The judge who heard the case ruled heavily in my favor. I was able to keep the house and most of the belongings. It was not an amicable split. Elaine was so angry she refused to pay her attorney.

The judge asked if we knew of anyone who could be the moderator and oversee the division of property. Bill Knight was selected. The judge also told us to be cordial to each other. On the day the belongings were divided, Elaine removed a fondue set from a drawer, grabbed a fork, pointed it at me, and said, "I feel like sticking this up your—"

Before she could finish, Stormy interrupted, "That is not being cordial, Elaine."

We went our separate ways. I continued to cover the Mariners, and Elaine became a flight attendant for United. She moved to Boston. On September 11, 2001, she was assigned to be on a flight from Boston to Los Angeles, but she met a man on an earlier flight. He invited her to Texas, and she accepted. She switched schedules with her roommate. The flight Elaine was supposed to be on was flown into the World Trade Center.

Other than the divorce, the '96 season was much ado about nothing. Well, one other thing—there was an earthquake that rocked the Kingdome on May 2, my dad's seventy-sixth birthday.

I was off that night but had gone to the Kingdome early to gather some notes for a feature story I was writing. I went back to my home in Renton and was having a quiet evening with Elaine when the telephone rang.

Dave Aust, the Mariners public relations director, was calling to see if I could hurriedly return to the Kingdome and be the official scorer for that night's game against the Indians. The official scorer assigned to the game was a no-show.

The game was scheduled to start in about fifteen minutes, so I suggested that I watch the game on TV and call him with my scoring decisions. No problem ... until the seventh inning. All of a sudden, during a pitching change following an Edgar Martinez home run, my house started to shake as though a strong wind was coming through. It was weird.

My TV went blank for a couple of seconds, so I called Dave. He informed me that the game had been stopped. My ruling: error—God. I learned later that Kevin Cremin, the radio engineer, knew exactly what had happened and bolted from the radio booth.

The remainder of the game was postponed and, after an inspection by engineers, resumed the following night. The regular scorer returned, and I filled him in on all the plays that had happened the previous night. He received the sixty dollars or so for being the official scorer.

It was a season without a postseason, and the prospects for a new stadium did not look good. CEO John Ellis made it clear that without a new stadium, the Mariners could not exist in Seattle.

On the field, the Mariners finished second to the Texas Rangers in the AL West despite a career year by Ken Griffey Jr. and a sensational rookie debut by shortstop Alex Rodriguez. The dynamic duo led the offense to a league-leading 993 runs, four players scored at least 100 runs, and four had at least 100 RBIs.

Griffey hit forty-nine home runs and drove in a 140 runs. A-Rod batted .358 with thirty-six homers and 123 RBIs. Jay Buhner contributed forty-four home runs and 138 RBIs. And Edgar Martinez had a solid season, batting .327 with twenty-six home runs and 103 RBIs.

Alex batted second, ahead of Griffey, and was superb. A-Rod and I became, I thought, pretty good friends. We talked about his development as a kid growing up in Miami. He was cordial at all times during the season and was even nice to my daughter, Katy, who wanted to meet him when she visited that summer.

Meanwhile, ace left-hander Randy Johnson, 18–2 in '95, went 5–0 in fourteen starts before being felled by a back injury that eventually required surgery. His presence was sorely missed. The pitching staff ERA of 5.21 was the highest in franchise history. It was amazing the Mariners were in the playoff hunt until the final weekend of the season.

A single-season attendance record (2.7 million) was established. Seattle had become a baseball town!

A-Rod was voted by his peers the MLB Player of the Year. I had nothing to do with that award but agreed with the choice. Alex was the best player in the major leagues that season, but was he the AL MVP?

It was one of those strange years when the MVP was loaded with candidates. The Mariners had A-Rod and Junior. The Rangers' Juan Gonzalez batted .314, hit forty-four home runs, and drove in 140 runs for the AL West champions. Rafael Palmeiro hit thirty-nine home runs and drove in 142 runs for the playoff-bound Orioles.

As one of the two Seattle-area writers voting for the MVP award, I paid special attention to the leading candidates throughout September. In a Sunday story in the *Times,* A-Rod told Bob Finnigan that he did not think he would win the MVP award. "I am not even the most valuable player on my team; how can I be the MVP of the league?" the rookie said, referring to Griffey.

I wasn't sure where I would place either Griffey or Rodriguez on my ballot, which listed ten players. I had decided that one of them would be number one and the other number three on my ballot. To get a better idea, when the Mariners were on road trips I would ask the opposing manager who they thought was the Mariners' MVP. I asked skippers Mike Hargrove (Indians), Tom Kelly (Twins), and Art Howe (Athletics). All said Ken Griffey Jr.

I also compared the all-important September statistics of my four leading candidates: Junior, A-Rod, Gonzalez, and Palmeiro.

- Griffey batted .300 with eight home runs and twenty-five RBIs.
- A-Rod batted .275 with three home runs and thirteen RBIs.
- Gonzalez batted .245 with six home runs and twenty-one RBIs.
- Palmeiro batted .286 with eight home runs and twenty-one RBIs.

As decision day approached, I decided to vote Griffey first, Gonzalez second, A-Rod third, and Palmeiro fourth.

During the final weekend in Oakland, A-Rod called me over to his locker and mentioned that Finnigan "dissed me in the MVP vote." That meant Finnigan did not vote Rodriguez number one. I had already voted but didn't mention who I had voted for and in what order. It was, after all, a secret ballot. Or so I thought.

A-Rod won practically every offensive award during the off-season. And then came the MVP announcement. He was so sure he would win that he invited a Miami-area TV crew to his house.

Gonzalez won. A-Rod finished second, three points behind Gonzalez. Griffey was third.

If either Finnigan or I had voted Rodriguez number one, he would have won. He also would have won if John Hickey, who covered the Athletics, had voted A-Rod third instead of seventh. I requested a copy of Hickey's ballot and saw that he originally had A-Rod third on his ballot but crossed out his name and inserted Rangers catcher Ivan Rodriguez, who had been seventh. The flip-flop would eventually harm Hickey's relationship with Rodriguez.

My sports editor, Glenn Drosendahl, assigned me to do a story on why I had voted the way I did. I used the quote attributed to A-Rod in the *Times* story and the information I had gathered from other major-league managers. It didn't make any difference with the young shortstop. As far as he was concerned, the writers who covered the team in Seattle were responsible for him not winning the MVP award in 1996.

Laura Vecsey, the *Post-Intelligencer* sports columnist, wrote that the two Seattle voters were afraid not to vote for Griffey. That was, on my part at least, total nonsense. My respect for her went into the garbage can. The least she could have done was ask me before writing it. She didn't.

Later on in the off-season, Rodriquez was selected as the Sports Star of the Year Award–winner at the *Post-Intelligencer*'s annual banquet. He thanked the fans for their support, adding this caveat: "I'm glad Finnigan and Street didn't vote for this award."

Little did he know that I did vote for the Sports Star of the Year. How I voted remains a secret. In the end, I learned what a lot of people have discovered: Alex Rodriguez is as phony as a three-dollar bill.

The highlight of that off-season was going (alone) to Kauai for two weeks of some much-needed R&R.

Chapter 22

1997: A New Stadium Is on the Way

A proposal to increase the sales tax by .01 percent in King County failed near the end of the September to remember in 1995, but a special session of the state legislature the following month authorized a different funding package for a new stadium.

The deal assured that the Mariners would remain in Seattle for at least another thirty years, and the person most responsible for the popularity of the team and getting a retractable-roof outdoor facility in the first place was front and center.

On March 8, 1997, more than thirty thousand fans showed up to watch Ken Griffey Jr. help break ground for the new ballpark located south of the Kingdome. Safeco Field would become known as "the house Griffey built."

I missed the ceremony, because I had my hands full with the daily duties associated with covering the team during spring training in Peoria, Arizona.

The intense competition between the *Post-Intelligencer* and the *Times* increased when the joint operation agreement was altered. In exchange for giving the *Post-Intelligencer* the rights to post stories on the Internet, the *Times* would move from being an afternoon publication to a morning paper, butting heads with my paper. The *Times* would hold exclusive publication rights for the Sunday *Seattle Times–Post-Intelligencer*.

My sports editor, Glenn Drosendahl, was entering his second full year in the position. For the most part, he was a nice guy. But one strike against him—in my book, anyway—was that he didn't care much for baseball. His preferences were the Seahawks, women's basketball, and the *Post-Intelligencer* Sports Star of the Year banquet.

He scored a bunch of points with me when he wrote a letter to Cathy Henkel, the sports editor of the *Times,* and requested that Bob Finnigan no longer be allowed to go through pregame workouts and, hygiene notwithstanding, shower with the players.

Finnie's world was crushed when his traveling equipment bag was retired.

Glenn was my third sports editor at the *Post-Intelligencer.* Bill Knight ran the department like a pro until 1992, when thirty-something-year-old Tim Kelly arrived. He brought some great ideas and a whip with him. Kelly wasn't John Rawlings–like, but he demanded good work from everyone. He told me, "I don't expect to get beat on any story!" I was afraid to ask what would happen if that happened.

While I felt comfortable that I could hold my own, Finnigan was a good reporter and was going to break some stories. After twenty-five years in the business, I knew better than Kelly that there wasn't a beat writer in newspaper history that broke *every* story.

I survived the Kelly years.

When it came to covering newsworthy events, he was at the top of his game. When Nancy Kerrigan was whacked on the knee prior to the '92 Winter Olympics and Portland-based Tonya Harding's husband became a suspect, Kelly sent *Post-Intelligencer* sports reporter Angelo Bruscas to Portland to sniff around. Angelo did a fantastic job of coming up with some terrific stories.

When I was in Chicago covering the AL playoffs in 1993, Michael Jordan announced that he was retiring from basketball. Kelly called and told me to rent a car, drive to the Bulls practice facility, and cover the press conference for the *Post-Intelligencer.* It was a terrific assignment. I went, I covered, I wrote.

That was in the morning, and in the afternoon, I covered the White Sox playoff game against the Blue Jays. It was a long day but one of the most memorable doubleheaders of my career.

Kelly was also a bit quirky.

Before leaving for spring training in '95, he told me that I should cook some of my own meals. It was, he figured, a way to save the company some money. I could see an occasional home-cooked meal, but as I told him, "The best way for me to stay healthy throughout spring training is to eat out, not cook for myself."

Tim decided to make a trip to camp. He arrived in the early afternoon, and I met him at the condo I had rented for the spring. He had a shopping list prepared for the meal he was going to prepare that night—spaghetti and meatballs.

He returned later with all the goodies and a bottle of red wine. He searched all the drawers but couldn't find a corkscrew. Finally, he asked if I would go to a store and buy a cheap one. I purchased the cheapest one I could find—a seventy-nine-cent piece of junk. But I figured it must work or the store wouldn't carry it. I returned to the condo and started to take the corkscrew out of the package, somewhat aggressively.

"Wait!" he yelled. "Don't ruin the packaging. When we're finished, we can put it back and take it back to the store for a refund." I kid you not.

As far as I know, the corkscrew is still in a drawer in that condo.

And where is Tim Kelly? He was shuffled off to Beaumont, Texas, in the summer of '95, where he still resides.

Meanwhile, the Mariners were off and running to a second AL West Division championship. The team won a franchise-best ninety regular season games, more than 3 million fans attended games at the Kingdome, and five Mariners—Griffey, Edgar Martinez, Alex Rodriguez, Randy Johnson and little Joey Cora—were selected to the All-Star team.

Johnson became the franchise's first twenty-game winner, and I became the vice-president of the Baseball Writers' Association of America (BBWAA).

I had been an active member of the BBWAA since 1972, serving on several committees. The San Francisco–Oakland chapter was one of the most active in terms of attendance at the annual chapter luncheon used to select officers.

Seattle was just the opposite. For whatever reason, the Seattle chapter rarely had a quorum at the precamp meeting. One of those occasions occurred in '97, the year it was the Seattle chapter's turn to select the national vice-president. The selection deadline was in June, and when nothing had been done, Jack O'Connell called Harland Beery, the secretary-treasurer of the Seattle chapter, and reminded him of the fast-approaching deadline.

Beery contacted Bob Sherwin, the chapter chairman, and they decided that because I had been the most active member of the chapter, attending BBWAA meetings during the All-Star Game and World Series (events Bob Finnigan rarely attended), and had been a member of the BBWAA the longest, I should be the Seattle selection. I was asked to serve as the national vice-president and accepted the offer.

The vice-president of the BBWAA doesn't do much. It's a quiet position, for the most part. No one in the Seattle chapter including Finnigan said a word about the selection, although he might not have known anything about it.

On the field, as good as the Mariners were, they finished short of their ultimate goal—winning the World Series. The wildcard Orioles delivered a crushing blow by winning the first two games, 9–3, at the Kingdome, hammering Randy Johnson and Jamie Moyer, a seventeen-game winner during the regular season. The series shifted to Baltimore, where the Mariners won game three but lost game four, ending the division series in five games.

It was a tough way to end the season, especially one that had so much Fall Classic promise attached to it.

Chapter 23

1998: Time for a Career Change

The Baseball Writers' Association of America gavel passed into my hands during the 1997 winter meetings, where I assumed the duties of president of the BBWAA, a once-in-a-career honor.

There were twenty-six chapters in the BBWAA at the time. Each city had its own chapter, while multiteam cities like San Francisco/Oakland, New York, Chicago, and Los Angeles had two-team chapters. The national officers are determined each year on a rotation basis.

Each local chapter selects a national vice-president who becomes the national president the following year. As president, I selected a four-man board of directors and anticipated a quiet, uneventful season.

I miscalculated badly in what turned out to be a very eventful 1998 season.

I decided to report to camp earlier than usual that spring. The game plan was to fly to Phoenix; rent a car; drive to Boulder City, Nevada, to visit my brother, Lary; play some golf; and return to Phoenix a couple of days later, meeting up with Bob Melnyk, a good friend and my insurance broker, and his good friend Pete. We planned to play two rounds of golf before the Mariners pitchers and catchers reported. They were scheduled to arrive in Phoenix the same day I returned from Boulder City.

After getting my luggage, I took a shuttle to the Hertz car rental facility. I had made reservations for a compact car, but the attendant offered me a midsize for the same price. It was a no-brainer upgrading to a brand-new, bright red Ford Mustang.

The drive to Boulder City went well. The golf also went well. I beat Lary. The drive back to Phoenix went not so well. Somewhere south of Wikiup and north of Wickenburg, Arizona, I was minding my own business on the winding two-lane road when a small car suddenly came out of nowhere, obviously out of control. It crossed the centerline, and I had no time to slam on the brakes or play dodge-the-car.

The car slammed into the front side of my rented Mustang. The airbag deployed, and when I came to my senses a few seconds later, my car was off to the right side of the road and the front tire was protruding through the floorboard, trapping my left ankle against the foot brake. I couldn't dislodge my foot, and panic set in.

I pulled harder and finally freed my foot. I tried to open the door to get out, but it was jammed. The window that had been there was gone, broken into tiny pieces on the seat, the floor, and (I found later) in the left pocket of my jogging suit top.

As I finished climbing out of the window, a woman came running up to me yelling, "I need a hug! I need a hug!"

It was the driver of the other car, and I did not offer her a hug.

The entire front of her car, a small Chevy, was missing. The engine was in a million pieces, it seemed, on the pavement. About that time, a car pulling a trailer rounded the corner and pulled to a stop off the right side of the road.

A woman emerged from the passenger side, screaming at the lady needing a hug, "I knew you were going to kill someone!"

Apparently, the woman who had hit me had been driving like a maniac as she passed one car after another, going much faster than she should have been going.

I called 911, and the nice woman asked if I was okay. I spent the next forty-five minutes or so waiting for a state police officer and ambulance to show up. In the meantime, blood trickled from underneath my left plants leg. The nice woman noticed and went to her trailer for a bandage.

She came back a few minutes later. She couldn't find a bandage but thought Kotex would do the job. She put it on my ankle, where the blood was coming from, and the bleeding subsided. I told her, "I guess I should be thankful you don't use tampons."

She laughed, and we waited for assistance. A patrol car, ambulance, and helicopter all arrived about the same time. The bad woman was airlifted to Kingman, Arizona, some two hours away by car. The chopper and the ambulance both offered me a ride. But both were going in the opposite direction I was, so I declined. I notified the Hertz folks about the accident, and they told me to leave the car where it was and they would arrange to have it towed back to Phoenix.

Before the nice couple with the trailer left, she pointed at my red Mustang and said, "Look what's leaning against the back bumper of your car."

It was a white wooden cross. I have absolutely no idea to this day how it got there. Perhaps it was the calling card of my guardian angel.

The patrolman offered me a ride to the Wickenburg Hospital, and I accepted. He was a cool dude to do that, and it saved me a lot of hassle. I called my insurance agent's wife at the insurance agency in Renton and informed her what had happened and asked her to let her husband know that I would not meet them at the predetermined time after all.

My wound was mended at the hospital, but I still needed a ride to Phoenix. A shuttle of some sort was due to leave Wickenburg, and I was able to get a ride. I finally arrived at the Enterprise Car Rental, where Bob and Pete were, and off we went to the condo that I had rented for the spring.

The good news was that I was not badly hurt. The bad news was that I was hurt badly enough that I couldn't play golf the next day as planned. I tried, but the ankle hurt too much. Prior to our round, we drove to the Hertz place to get my suitcase and golf clubs, which were still in the totaled Mustang.

We drove in and noticed a blue tarp being placed over the red Mustang. I asked one of the men if he had the car keys so I could get into the trunk. He didn't. We looked inside the car, and lying on the floor of the passenger side were the keys, still in the ignition that had been on the side of the steering column. It must have been quite a collision.

I asked about the blue tarp.

"We always cover the car when there's a fatality," a worker said.

Camp opened three days later, and I was on the job from day one.

There was somewhat of a cloud hanging over the Mariners' side of the Peoria Sports Complex. Ace left-hander Randy Johnson was entering the final year of his contract, and unless he was resigned before the July 31 nonwaiver trading deadline, he most likely would be traded.

I had known Randy for nine years, and we had gotten along well. There were certain rules he demanded, like not talking to anyone on the day before or the day of his starts, but that was no problem. There were plenty of other players to interview or simply shoot the breeze with.

Of all the pitchers I covered from 1971 through 1997, Randy Johnson was the best—better than Catfish, Vida, Langston, and Mike Moore. Randy was tops, by far. Covering his games in the '90s must have been like covering Sandy Koufax in the 1960s. Randy was dominating practically every start he made.

I did not, however, cover Johnson's no-hitter against the Tigers in 1990. It came on a Saturday night, and because the *Post-Intelligencer* did not publish on Sunday, I took the night off. I vowed then that I would never miss another Randy Johnson start.

But there were a few of his starts in the '98 season that I wished I had missed.

One of them came against the Athletics in Oakland. Jay Buhner had given the Mariners a 2–0 lead in the second inning with a home run, but Johnson surrendered four runs in the bottom of the inning. It appeared to me that he was just going through the motions.

His record fell to 5–6. Six weeks remained until the trade deadline. It had been a difficult season for Johnson, the Mariners, and manager Lou Piniella.

Trade rumors were blowing in the wind from all directions, increasing in force when it became obvious that a contract extension was not forthcoming. It was obvious that Johnson wanted out of Seattle, and he would often ask Lou for a trade-rumor update. The skipper wanted to keep his best pitcher focused and productive. More than once, Lou said, "The better you pitch, the better chances you have of being traded."

After one of those meetings, Lou told the media, "Sometimes I feel like Madeline Albright."

Among his many strong suits, Lou was one of the funniest people I ever met. He was full of great George Steinbrenner stories and enjoyed telling them, especially at a dinner table with the media. We ate it up, and regardless how many times we heard the same story, it never changed and was always hilarious.

Lou also had a will to win. A strong will to win. I honestly believe that the only thing worse than absorbing a loss was absorbing a loss to the Yankees. From the moment Piniella became the Mariners manager, games between the Mariners and Yankees were as good as it gets in a regular season, let alone in a postseason. As a player with the Yankees, Lou was one of the most popular among the fans. They loved his fire, his desire, and his charisma.

In Seattle, fans loved all of the above and his tantrums.

If the Olympic Games had a base-throwing event, Lou would win the gold medal. If there were a cap-kicking event, he'd win that one too. Want to see an argument between manager and umpire? Find a Piniella clip, and you'll be entertained for many minutes.

Of all the managers I covered, Lou and Dick Williams are at the top of the list at 1 and 1A. They were polar opposites in many ways but carbon copies when it came to playing the game the right way. Players would run through brick walls for both of them and ask questions later.

Lou had a big heart and a queasy stomach. On several occasions, usually when the team was playing well, Jay Buhner would play a little trick on his friend and skipper. Buhner could barf on cue. He would put some milk in his mouth, walk up to an unsuspecting Piniella, and do his vomiting act. Poor Lou would almost lose it.

Meanwhile, the Big Unit's performance that day in Oakland hit a nerve with me. I decided to write a letter to Randy via the *Post-Intelligencer*. My message was this: you are not living up to your contract, you are letting your teammates down, and you should act like a professional and do the job that you're being paid quite well to do.

The letter was displayed at the top of the *Post-Intelligencer* sports section.

I was sleeping in my hotel room at the Fullerton Marriott when the phone rang at a little after 8:00 a.m. Johnson's agent, Barry Meister, was on the other end of the line from Chicago, and he was not a happy camper. He yelled at me for a good (bad?) ten or so minutes before I finally had a chance to explain why I had written what I had written.

I think the explanation fell on deaf ears. I learned later in the day from the *Post-Intelligencer* receptionist that Meister had called the *Post-Intelligencer* switchboard at 8:00 a.m. sharp and said, "I just got off the phone with Jim Street and forgot to get his phone number. I need to ask him something and was wondering if you had his phone number."

He lied, and she gave him the number.

Several MLB scouts attending the Angels-Mariners game that night saw the article. As was a custom, the visiting PR representative had a clipping of that day's stories. Several scouts praised the story, saying it was right on. They had seen the same things I had.

Randy did not say anything to me for several days. Finally, when the team was in Arizona and he and I were alone in the visiting clubhouse at Bank One Ballpark, he came up and said, "I read your article, and I am holding myself back from punching you in the mouth."

I told him to go ahead if it made him feel better. I also said that I could use the money.

That obviously damaged the friendly relationship we had, but on a bright note, we have since settled our differences and he remains the most dominating pitcher I ever had the pleasure of covering. He's a slam-dunk first-ballot Hall of Famer.

Also in June, I received a letter in the mail from one Bob Finnigan. He had written a two-page fabrication accusing me of orchestrating my appointment as the BBWAA national president. It included, among other things, reasons why he should have been selected including the fact he was the dean of Seattle Mariners beat reporters, etc., etc., etc. I digested the letter and responded to it, basically calling him a nutcase and pointing out that none of what he said was correct. I needed fewer than two pages, and before long, I received another letter apologizing and acknowledging that he should eat some crow.

One of the perks of being BBWAA president is getting to participate in the Hall of Fame ceremonies in Cooperstown, New York, in July. I invited my kids to join me, and they happily accepted. I flew them to

Seattle, and we took a flight to Albany, where a van from the Otesaga Hotel met us.

The scenic drive must have taken a little more than an hour. What a spectacular drive it was.

We arrived in Cooperstown in the late afternoon and checked into the hotel, sharing the spectacular facility full of Hall of Fame players like Sandy Koufax, Warren Spahn, Hank Aaron, Stan Musial, and Yogi Berra, a teammate of Scott and Katy's grandfather with the Yankees.

Besides dinners, breakfasts, and lunches, the Hall of Fame festivities included golf and tennis tournaments. I played golf, and Hall of Fame pitcher Juan Marichal was in my foursome. Katy and Scott played mixed doubles in the tennis tourney. Katy won first place, receiving one good-looking glass trophy.

When the kids slept, I practiced my speeches. My job for the induction ceremonies was twofold: give the welcome address and introduce Sam Lacy, the Spink Award recipient. The speeches went off with only a glitch or two, but not bad from a kid from little Dorris, California (population one thousand).

Several days after returning home, I was writing a story about Randy Johnson's trade to the Astros for pitchers Freddy Garcia and John Halama and infielder Carlos Guillen. The Mariners had a 48–60 record and hopes for another postseason playoff berth were long gone.

But the season continued, nonetheless, and when I arrived in Cleveland on August 25 for the opener of a three-game series against the Indians, I had three phone messages: one from Katy Feeney of the National League office, another one from the public relations director of the Colorado Rockies, and one from *Rocky Mountain News* reporter Tracy Ringolsby.

All of them addressed the same topic: A Denver sports columnist had been caught taking a bottle of "andro" out of Dante Bichette's locker at Coors Field.

My first call was to Feeney, the daughter of former NL president Chub Feeney. She explained what had happened, told me the Rockies had already lifted the columnist's credential, and said she wanted to know what action the BBWAA was going to take.

My next call was to Jack Lang, the former longtime BBWAA secretary-treasurer. I was aware of only one other instance when a reporter had his BBWAA credential suspended. I discussed the situation, and Jack recommended that I contact the board of directors, which I did. But first I called Jack O'Connell, the current secretary-treasurer, and informed him.

The board of directors all agreed that we should suspend the columnist's BBWAA card for the remainder of the season.

I felt satisfied that we covered all the bases and were thorough with our process in determining what action to take. I thought we were fair and felt especially good that a move among several general managers to close clubhouses to the media before games had been cut off at the pass.

There was no doubt in my mind that if the BBWAA did not respond the way it did, the general managers were going to feel they needed to limit the media's access to the players prior to games. That might work in the NFL but would not work in MLB.

I discovered much later that Bichette had, in fact, given the columnist permission to take the item from his locker, which led to the case being settled out of court.

Later on that season, Ken Bunting, the *Post-Intelligencer* managing editor, came up with what he considered a brilliant idea. Ellis Conklin, a features department writer, was an avid baseball fan. Bunting decided that it would be terrific for the newspaper to have a fan cover the Mariners beat. Conklin became the Mariners beat writer for the upcoming home stand, and I was temporarily reassigned to the features department.

It made absolutely no sense to me, but who was I to question someone as brilliant as Bunting?

Conklin could not handle the deadline pressure, and the *Post-Intelligencer* had to send another reporter to the Kingdome every night to get player and manager quotes for the frazzled Conklin. The brilliant idea lasted less than two weeks. I was back on the beat. Bunting's actions were on a list of reasons why assistant sports editor Dwight Perry left the *Post-Intelligencer* and took a job at the rival *Seattle Times*. I am not sure what Bunting is doing these days, but driving a garbage truck somewhere would be a good guess.

And you wonder why newspapers are going belly-up?

Dan O'Brien, the former president and general manager of the Mariners, had become the CEO of USA Baseball in Tucson, Arizona, and our paths had crossed in the spring of '98. We chatted, and he asked if I might be interested in working for his organization.

He gave me his business card, and I put it in my wallet.

Bunting made me seriously consider leaving the newspaper business. A few weeks later, I was invited to Bob Sherwin's fiftieth birthday party in Sammamish, Washington. We knew each other in San Francisco, when he as an assistant sports editor at the *Examiner* and I was a reporter at the San Jose *Mercury-News*. He had moved to Seattle months before me and, among other things, was the Mariners' backup baseball writer.

Bob and his wife, Charlotte, wanted me to meet Becky Marsh, an interior designer who had helped them on their new house. We met at the party, and I thought she was really a nice woman. But in the back of my mind was USA Baseball in Tucson.

As August turned to September, the team was struggling, and there was some scuttlebutt in the great Northwest that manager Lou Piniella's job was in jeopardy. I didn't believe it, but I called club president Chuck Armstrong for a comment.

As expected, he said the rumor was ridiculous and Lou's job was not in jeopardy. I wrote a note about it for the next day's paper, a short piece that was not a big deal—in my mind.

When I walked into the manager's office at Candlestick Park that afternoon, I noticed immediately that Piniella was not in a good mood. I soon discovered why Lou was so blue.

"If you want to know something about my job security, ask me!" he said, the words dripping with sarcasm.

Several of his coaches were in the room at the time. Lou turned and walked out. I didn't have a chance to say much of anything.

Later on, when we were alone, I said, "Lou, in the future I would really appreciate it if we could talk one-on-one when you want to criticize my work. Furthermore, I don't tell you how to manage, so I don't expect you to tell me how to do my job."

No harm, no foul, and we remained, I thought, pretty good friends.

The Mariners' season mercifully ended on schedule, and after a brief vacation, I eventually returned to work and resumed covering the University of Washington women's basketball team.

The University of Washington football coach was on the verge of being fired, and all sorts of rumors were circulating. One of them indicated that the coach was having an affair with Sunny Smallwood, the Husky women's assistant basketball coach.

I reported to work at the *Post-Intelligencer* and was called into sports editor Glenn Drosendahl's office.

"I want you to go and ask Sunny Smallwood if she's having an affair with the football coach," he said.

"Are you serious?" I responded.

"Yes, I am."

I drove to the university, found Sunny Smallwood in an office and said, "I really don't want to ask you this, but I have been told I have to do it—are you having an affair with the football coach?"

It was not a pleasant exchange. I felt horrible. Was this what journalism was all about?

The coach was fired, the stories came out, and there was not one mention of an affair. Like most rumors, this one was stupid and unfounded. But I had to lower myself and ask a question that never should have been asked in the first place.

I began thinking that now was the time to get out the newspaper business.

I called O'Brien and pursued the USA Baseball job. Four months later, I was working for him at USA Baseball in Tucson, Arizona.

It meant, among other things, that the introductory meeting I had with Becky Marsh would be just that—a meeting with some friendly conversation. As I learned later, Becky asked Bob about me. He said I had moved to Tucson.

"I didn't want to marry him," she said. "I just wanted a dinner date."

Chapter 24

1999–2000: Two Jobs in Two Years

My Newcastle house sold so quickly there never was a For Sale sign put into the ground. I took that to be a good sign. A month or so later, I embarked on my new world—as website manager for USA Baseball.

The organization had a website, but it wasn't very good. My job was to improve it. Dan O'Brien was a terrific person, experienced in baseball, and had the organization on the way up. The United States Olympic Committee spent a lot of money on other sports but not so much on baseball. Baseball was a big success in the Olympic Games. USA Baseball also had national and junior national teams. There were a lot of great stories to write.

I arrived in Tucson at the end of April, purchased a house, went to work at the offices located at Hi Corbett Field, and expected to play a role in the growth of USA Baseball. Not quite.

First of all, Dan didn't notify any of the other workers there that I had been hired. I was like an unwanted child among most of the employees. But one who was glad to see me was Jeff Odenwald. He was the marketing director with tons of professional experience including stints with the Mariners, Reds, Cubs, and Tigers.

He knew his stuff and only recently had landed lucrative financial deals with Texaco and US West, the major sponsors for USA Baseball, for the next couple of years at least.

Dan was nearing retirement age—actually, he already was beyond retirement age—and the marketing deals Jeff made put him in the driver's seat to become the next CEO of USA Baseball.

That did not sit well with much of the staff O'Brien had hired. Paul Seiler, for example, had his sights set on the CEO position. I did not know that Seiler and his band of brothers were plotting to take command of USA Baseball.

Within one month, I knew I had made a huge career mistake. I had gotten the cold shoulder from Seiler and his coconspirators. Jeff and Dan were the only ones in the office that showed any interest in what I was doing there.

The national team began playing games in June, thank goodness, so there was something I could get my hands around. I wrote stories to post on the website. The national team, which included right-handed pitcher Mark Prior, went on a tour of the West Coast and mid-America.

The team might as well travel, because home attendance at Hi Corbett Field was dismal. "Crowds" of fifty to a hundred were the rule. I would joke with Bob Thompson, the public address announcer, that he was heard by fewer people than any PA announcer in the history of sports. He didn't disagree. Bob and his wife Joanne became, and still are, great friends.

The national team tour ended with a game in St. Paul, Minnesota. It so happened that the Mariners were in Minneapolis to play the Twins, so I arranged for the USA Baseball team to get tickets. The players were allowed on the field to watch pregame batting practice. Among the Mariners hitters was Tiger Woods, who had been invited by Ken Griffey Jr. Tiger had some difficulty getting the ball out of the batting cage.

Upon our return to Tucson, Dan assigned me to accompany the junior national team to the world championships in Taiwan in August of '99. That team included shortstop Jeff Baker, who is now in the major leagues, and fifteen-year-old catcher Joe Mauer. The minimum age was supposed to be sixteen, but Mauer was so good that he had to be on the team.

The USA won the world championship. Things were looking up.

But a few weeks after the junior team returned to Tucson, the proverbial roof fell in—and I'm not talking about ceiling tiles falling into seats. Dan O'Brien was fired as the CEO.

The next day, I was called into Paul Seiler's office.

"We are going to let you go," he said. "I wish I had gotten to know you better."

I told him he could have if he hadn't passed on several lunch invitations I had made. I put the severance check in my pocket, walked out of the office, went home, and consumed a bottle of wine.

The phone rang later, and it was Jeff Odenwald. He also had been fired.

For the first time in my life, I went on unemployment. It was demeaning but necessary. The days were long; the nights were longer. All I could think was, *Well, you sure got yourself into a mess now. How are you going to get out of it?*

A call to my guardian angel went unanswered.

But my older brother, Ron, called. He asked if I had any frequent flyer miles remaining. I checked, and I did. He suggested that we meet in Toulouse, France. He had a terrific job at Qualcomm in San Diego and was going to be teaching some students in Argentina the ins and outs of CDMA. Don't ask me what that means.

Anyway, he would be traveling from Buenos Aires to Paris and then to Toulouse. We would meet there and share his hotel room. It was a nice gesture and perhaps a reciprocal gesture for the hotel rooms I had shared with him in such places at Toronto and Kansas City when I covered the Mariners. Those were good times, and we had fun.

I booked a United Airlines flight and headed to France.

I arrived a few hours before Ron and spent time touring the city. I fell in love with the place. We met, exchanged stories of our trips, and hit the sack. The following day, we had breakfast and went our separate ways. He went to work; I went to play. I toured the city, and although it was cold, it was much better than the sun in Tucson.

A couple of days into the trip, Ron and I were having breakfast at the hotel. I was looking for a way to spend the day, so I asked our waitress for a suggestion. She said Lourdes was a fine tourist site. It was up in the mountains, and I wasn't sure how I was going to get there. I noticed that she didn't have a ring on her finger and suggested that she could be my tour guide in Lourdes.

She declined, almost running from the table, and we never saw her again.

I decided that Lourdes would have to wait, and I booked a train trip to Paris instead. It was a day trip. The train left early and returned late, but that was okay. The ride through French wine country, the Bordeaux region, was spectacular. I saw many farmhouses and imagined US troops spending nights there during World War II. At least my imagination was still working.

I managed to get around Paris without knowing a word of French. The people were friendly, and I was the cordial American. I don't how much of Paris I saw, but it was a lot. I walked, I rode buses, I went on a boat ride. I didn't climb the Eiffel Tower but sure was impressed with the size of the structure. I didn't go into the museums, but they were magnificent from the outside.

I returned to Toulouse, arriving early in the morning. I met my brother for breakfast. The waitress that we had met a few days earlier was a no-show—for the third straight day!

Meanwhile, Qualcomm stock quadrupled. Ron made a bunch of bucks in one day. Good for him.

I returned to Tucson to face reality and begin "networking," the process of contacting anyone and everyone you know who might know about a job opening. Not surprisingly, nothing much happened over the Christmas holidays of '99.

A new century began the same way the last one ended—with me looking for a job. I remembered that Greg Brown, a former colleague at the *Post-Intelligencer,* was doing a website for Alex Rodriguez. I called Ken Griffey Jr.'s agent, Brian Goldberg and asked if Junior had a website.

He did have a website—with something called Athlete's Direct at Broadband Sports located in Los Angeles. Brian gave me a phone number. I called and was transferred to Ken Gurnick, one of the top dogs at Broadband Sports. He also was a former baseball writer, covering the Dodgers for the *Los Angeles Herald-Examiner.* We knew each other well.

He set up an interview with me in Santa Monica, California, and I drove over to LA, staying at a Holiday Inn near UCLA. I went to the Broadband Sports offices for the interview and returned to Tucson. A few days later, Gurnick called and offered me a job.

Broadband Sports was flush with cash, having received $60 million from investors. The plan was to go public to raise much more money, and part of my deal was thirty thousand shares. I would learn later that thirty thousand shares of nothing is nothing.

I found a place to live, a converted garage behind a nice house in Beverly Hills, for "only" nine hundred dollars a month. That was more than my house payment in Tucson. The landlord wanted me to sign a one-year lease. I explained that I wasn't positive that the job would last one year, so we worked out a deal where I would pay rent for three months and then receive a one-month grace period. If I was still there at the end of the grace period, I would sign a one-year lease effective that date.

Two weeks before the grace period ended, I was allowed to move back to Tucson and work out of my house. I never did work on Griffey's website, but I did thank Brian Goldberg many times for hooking me up with Broadband Sports.

Unfortunately, the company spent more money than it took in. Before long, the $60 million was gone, the public stock offering didn't materialize, and Broadband Sports went belly-up. I was at home in mid-November when Gurnick called.

"We're downsizing," he said, "and I have to let you go."

Oh, great—another Thanksgiving and Christmas without a job. I had two jobs in the first twenty-eight years of my career, and now I was looking for my third job in the past two years. I hadn't been this bummed since my first divorce.

Prior to my pink slip from Broadband Sports, I had spent a few days in Seattle in October. The Mariners had clinched a playoff spot on the final day of the 2000 season. Tim Hevly, the team's director of media relations, called and asked if I would be available to be an official scorer for the Mariners' home games if the team reached the AL Championship Series.

I received permission from my employer, and it was off to Seattle and Safeco Field, a facility I had never seen. When I walked into the plush park, I knew this was no Kingdome. Yankees right-hander Roger Clemens started the third game of the best-of-seven series and buzzed Alex Rodriguez with the first pitch. A-Rod was done for the day. He went hitless. But so did just about everyone else in the Mariners lineup.

Clemens took a no-hitter into the seventh inning. There had been only one postseason no-hitter in MLB history—Don Larsen's perfect game in the 1956 World Series. Might I be scoring the second one? Nope. Mariner outfielder Al Martin led off the seventh inning with a double to right field, barely out of the reach of Yankees first baseman Tino Martinez. It was the first and only hit of the game for the Mariners, who lost the game and fell into a three-games-to-one deficit. The Yankees won the series in six games. I thanked Tim for the scoring opportunity and returned to Seattle. A month later, I was looking for a new job.

In January of 2001, I returned to Seattle to visit some friends, among them Tim Hevly. I stopped by the Mariners offices, and Dan Wartelle, who worked in the PR department, told me that MLB was going to merge all existing team websites into one operation. It would be called MLB.com.

"I think they are going to hire entry-level people to do the writing," Dan said. "But if you are interested, I can give you the name of the guy heading the project."

That would be Dinn Mann.

Hall of Fame second baseman Joe Morgan (right)
gives some fielding tips to an A's beat reporter

The Mariners remained in Seattle, thanks to
the amazing talent of Ken Griffey Jr.

Beat writers Steve Buckley (left), Bob Finnigan (right)
flank the author and skipper Dick Williams

Randy Johnson was the most dominant starting
pitcher in Mariners franchise history

The author visits Monument Park at the old Yankee
Stadium prior to Mariners-Yankees game

Edgar Martinez retired as one of the most popular
and dependable players in franchise history

Former Giants manager Frank Robinson, a Hall of
Fame player, poses with SF media corps

Hall of Fame outfielder Reggie Jackson chats with the
author about the good ol' days in Oakland

As president of the BBWAA, being an official scorer for the '98 All-Star Game had a ring to it

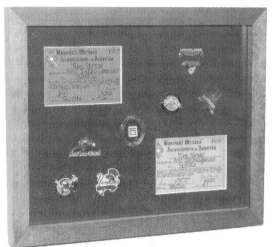

Cards and media pins for years as Vice President and President of the Baseball Writers Association of America

Story of the Mariners' plight published by The Sporting News

The 1972 World Series ring, compliments of Charles O. Finley

Namesake closer Huston Street
at the Oakland Colisum

Chapter 25

2001: A New Lease on Life

Armed with a name and phone number, I called Mann in New York. I introduced myself, discussed my work history, and asked him if there were any openings at MLB.com. I offered my services as the beat reporter for the Diamondbacks, Dodgers, Angels, or Padres—anywhere in the southwestern or western part of the country.

Dinn told me that he already had assembled a staff that included writers for all those teams. Ken Gurnick was the Dodgers beat writer for MLB.com.

I thanked him for his time, gave him my phone number, and asked him to call me if anything opened up. I was bummed. And still unemployed.

A couple of weeks later, on a Sunday, I was at my Tucson house watching NFL playoff games. The phone rang at about noon. Dinn Mann called to tell me that Eddie Mathews was in the final days or hours of his life and he needed a story ASAP to use as MLB.com's obituary.

Gulp! Sunday! ASAP! Turn off the TV and go to work.

The first call I made was to Irv Noren, my former father-in-law. I got some good information from him, as he was well aware of Mathews's career, having played in the same era. I knew Irv and Duke Snider were longtime friends, and my next call was to the Duke—my childhood idol.

He gave me some great stuff on Mathews and what it was like playing against him for several years when Eddie was with the Milwaukee

Braves and Duke with the Dodgers. I asked Duke if he had the phone numbers of any of Mathews's Braves teammates.

He gave me Warren Spahn's phone number. We chatted for several minutes, and I got more terrific info for my story. The Hall of Fame lefty gave me Johnny Logan's phone number. We must have talked for forty-five minutes, and the stories flowed from the Braves star shortstop that played alongside Eddie Mathews for many years. Interviewing Logan was like winning the lotto. There was so much great information.

Less than three hours after receiving the assignment, I e-mailed the lengthy story to MLB.com headquarters in New York. I called Dinn to make sure the story had arrived. It had. A few days later, on February 18, 2001, Eddie Mathews passed away. My first story for MLB.com appeared that day.

I received another phone call from Dinn asking me if I would consider going back to Seattle to cover the Mariners for MLB.com. The first word out of my mouth was "Absolutely!" I agreed to the salary offer, and it was good-bye unemployment.

The MLB.com office arranged for me to fly from Tucson to New York for a couple days of workshops. Groups of new employees went through training sessions. When I reached the MLB.com headquarters in the Chelsea section of town, I ran into Tom Singer, another former baseball writer. He had covered the Angels when I covered the Athletics. He had been hired as the Angels beat reporter.

As we prepared for our work session, there was a news flash from Seattle. An earthquake had hit the great Northwest. Dinn instructed me to leave the training session and call the Mariners to get a report on the status of Safeco Field.

All was well at the two-year-old stadium. I missed the training sessions that taught the new workers how to post their stories onto their respective websites. I was not at all upset by the fact that I would be working with Dan Wartelle, the Mariners website guru. I would cover the games, write the stories, and send them to Dan to be posted.

Even with the $30 million from MLB clubs, money was rather tight at MLB.com. Covering spring training would be hit-and-miss. I would commute to Peoria three days a week and gather enough information to write five or six stories a week.

When the team was on a road trip during the regular season, I would watch the game on TV, keep a play-by-play, and write an early game story, replacing it with a final story that included quotes that the home-team MLB.com reporter would send me.

The Mariners became the biggest story in the major leagues.

There had been some major roster changes during the two years I was away from the team. Gone were Ken Griffey Jr., traded to the Cincinnati Reds before the 1999 season, and Alex Rodriguez, who had opted for free agency and signed a $250 million contract with the division rival Rangers.

In their place were Ichiro Suzuki, an outfielder from Japan, and second baseman Bret Boone, trying to come back from a serious knee injury. Boonie was built like a truck. He had put on a lot of muscle from when I last saw him back in the mid-'90s before his trade to the Reds.

From the waist up, Suzuki looked like the skinny kid on the beach getting sand kicked in his face by the bullies. But his legs were disproportionately muscular. He preferred to be called by his first name only. And so he became Ichiro. His seven batting championships in Japan helped make him rock-star famous in the land of the rising sun.

He was so big that the Peoria Sports Complex was jammed with Japan-based media whose job was to monitor Ichiro's every move. The media kept track of every batting-practice swing he took and where every ball was hit. Afterward, they would interview the batting-practice pitcher for a report on Ichiro's batting-practice session.

This went on the entire spring. Every Japan sportswriter wrote about Ichiro every day! The Mariners had fifty-some other players in camp, but the only subject covered in Japan papers was Ichiro, who would meet with the horde of Japanese media after every practice and then, when he played, after every Cactus League game. I didn't envy the writers. I imagined what it would have been like to cover just Ken Griffey Jr. all those years.

One thing I noticed about Ichiro was how little he enjoyed being interviewed by the US media, even the beat writers. Whereas closer Kaz

Sasaki was one of the most outgoing players on the team, Ichiro was just the opposite. He hid his emotions well.

Returning to the Mariners beat for MLB.com also meant working in the same work space as Bob Finnigan. It didn't take long for me to realize that either he was in manager Lou Piniella's back pocket or vice versa. They were two peas in a pod.

I also noticed during the regular season that Finnie had toned down his old press-box antics of blasting players behind their backs and then patting them on their backs in the clubhouse. That is not to say, however, that he didn't blow a gasket now and then.

During a game against the Indians in Cleveland, Finnie became so upset with a call that the official scorer made (robbing one of his Mariners buddies of a hit) that he stood up and berated the scorer. Bart Swain, the Indians public-relations director, stood up, looked at Finnigan, and yelled, "Sit down and shut the fuck up!"

Finnie took a seat pronto. *Tacoma News-Tribune* beat writer Larry LaRue and I had a difficult time hiding our laughter.

Another time, at Safeco Field, Finnie was at his workstation talking on the phone. Well, yelling into the phone is more like it. He dropped more *f*-bombs during the conversation than you would have heard at a convention of foul-mouthed sailors.

He slammed the phone down.

"Who was that?" I asked.

"The bitch, Henkel!"

That would be his boss, *Times* sports editor Cathy Henkel.

Another time, also at Safeco Field, Finnie was irate with a *Times* technician. Finnie's computer, which had been turned on before he went downstairs to gather pregame notes, was dead when he returned.

The more Finnie talked, the angrier he got, dropping enough F-bombs to sink a ship. He was instructed to remove the battery and put it back in. The computer screen remained black.

Finally, fellow *Times* scribe Larry Stone noticed something.

"Uh, Finnie. Your computer is unplugged," Stone said.

A red-faced Finnigan calmly thanked the technician for his assistance and said he would try to fix the problem himself. He plugged the power cord into the electrical socket, and presto! The machine came to life.

But that was not the funniest thing I witnessed at Safeco Field in 2001.

A rookie reporter covering the Blue Jays was visiting Safeco for the first time and had no idea that the windows would be opened prior to the game. He had a new Apple computer painted a bright orange. I happened to walk past the area where visiting writers worked, and he was standing up, engaged in conversation with another writer.

All of a sudden, the window started going up. The look on his face was priceless.

"Stop! My computer!" he yelled.

He was so loud that the press-box attendant located at the opposite end of the press box heard the commotion and pushed the stop button. The writer had padlocked his computer to the window.

For the most part, I covered Mariners home games in '01, but I did make trips to Boston and New York, two of my favorite cities. Jim Banks, the west regional editor, asked me to travel to Oakland and meet with the two writers assigned to cover the Athletics. They were taking way too much time to file their postgame stories—up to four or five hours.

I met with them at the Coliseum and gave them some pointers. I suggested that they write about the game during the game (known in the business as *running*), put a topper on it at the end of the game, and embellish the story with player quotes later.

Neither one of them knew what I was talking about.

"This is not brain surgery," one of them said. "Anyone can do this."

But neither one of them could, and they were subsequently dismissed.

On the field, the Mariners bolted from the gate in '01 and never looked back. No Junior? No problem. No A-Rod? No problem. No Randy? No problem.

The Mariners were 20–4 on April 28 and on an eight-game winning streak. This band of brothers assembled by Pat Gillick was well on its way to some AL history. It was not a team of superstars as much as it was twenty-five players performing to the best of their abilities.

When the team won at home, players were allowed to bring their kids into the clubhouse afterward. Sasaki had a young son who was a hoot. A player would say a name, and the kid would demonstrate that player's batting stance.

The Mariners had thirty-one wins before their tenth loss and fifty-six wins before their twentieth defeat. They were 63–24 at the All-Star break, and practically the entire starting lineup was selected to play in the Midsummer Classic at Safeco Field. There were eight Mariners including four starters on the AL team.

Bob Finnigan wanted to be the ninth.

As the host team, the local chapter chairman serves as one of the official scorers. At the annual chapter meeting in January, Finnie nominated fellow *Times* reporter Bob Sherwin as chapter chairman, and he was voted in by the local writers.

A few weeks before the All-Star Game, Finnigan learned that the official scorers received All-Star rings just like the players. He went to Sherwin and explained that because he was the dean of Seattle baseball writers, he and not Sherwin should be the official scorer at the All-Star Game. Sherwin said he would think about it.

Sherwin decided to stick with protocol and handle the scoring duties. That made Finnie really angry. He eventually called Patrick Courtney in the MLB office in New York and requested a change—Sherwin to Finnigan. Courtney called Sherwin and left the ball in Bob's court.

"If you decide not to be an official scorer, we'll find someone else," Courtney said. "And it won't be Finnigan."

Sherwin was an official scorer and received an All-Star ring.

The Mariners kept winning, Ichiro kept piling up the hits, and second baseman Bret Boone had a season for the ages, setting personal highs for batting average (.331), home runs (thirty-seven) and RBIs (141). The team led the league in offense, defense, and pitching.

They won an AL record 116 games, tying the all-time MLB mark set by the Cubs in 1906. According to Baseball-Reference's calculation of team strength (by wins above replacement), the 2001 Mariners were the second-greatest team in MLB history, following only the 1939 New York Yankees.

The Mariners improved their record to 104–40 on September 10, 2001, with a victory over the Angels in Anaheim. The world changed forever the following morning as players and other team personnel were awakened by the horrific news that the twin towers at the World Trade Center had been attacked by hijacked commercial airplanes.

Play resumed eight days later, but there was something wrong. The players weren't nearly as sharp as they had been before the seven-day hiatus. They lost a season-high four straight games from September 20 to 23, losing a series for the first and only time during the amazing season.

The Mariners eliminated the Indians in a tough five-game division series, but the Yankees won four of the five games played in the AL Championship Series. After the Mariners lost the first two games of the series, played at Safeco Field, Piniella guaranteed that the series would return to Seattle for game six and game seven if needed.

The mood of the team really went into the dumps following a visit to the area near Ground Zero. It had been more than a month since the terrorist attack, but the smell of ash was still in the air. I had gone to the disaster area that same morning with MLB.com colleague Carrie Muskat. It was a mind-boggling experience.

The series did not return to Seattle as promised. The Mariners won just one of the three games played in Yankee Stadium, losing the best-of-seven series in five games. Of all Mariners teams before and after this juggernaut, this was the one that seemed it was going to give Seattle its first World Series.

But it was not to be.

Ichiro won the MVP and Rookie of the Year Awards, the first player since Fred Lynn to do it. The Mariners drew a record 3.5 million fans including fifty-four sellouts.

Times were good, and it was time for me to get better acquainted with Becky.

Chapter 26

2002: The Best Phone Call I Ever Made

The unofficial kickoff to a new baseball season occurs at the end of January, when the Mariners stage their two-day FanFest celebration at Safeco Field.

I left my Tucson home with more than covering the annual event on my mind. I had decided that I would try to reconnect with Becky Marsh. My first call was to Bob Sherwin. He had introduced us a couple of years earlier at his fiftieth birthday party, and I asked him if he knew whether Becky had gotten married, had a boyfriend, or had moved away. He said, "No," "Not that I know of," and "No."

I asked for her telephone number, and Bob said he would make sure his wife Charlotte talked to Becky before giving out the number and that he would get back to me.

Bob called me back before I returned to Tucson with Becky's telephone number. I called, and her teenage son, Brad, answered. Before I had a chance to say hello to Becky, Brad accidentally hung up on me.

However, Becky was aware that I would be calling her, and she called me back. We had a nice conversation and agreed to chat later. I returned to Tucson to prepare for the opening of spring training, making occasional calls to Becky.

Camp opened and most of our contact was via e-mail. It became pretty much a daily ritual throughout spring training. We connected and developed the early stages of a relationship via the Internet.

Meanwhile, at the Peoria Sports Complex, the Mariners were extremely upbeat from their record 116-win season. The disappointment of not winning, or even reaching, the World Series in 2001 was in their collective rearview mirror. It was time to move on.

Manager Lou Piniella returned for his tenth season. His 747 wins entering the season were far and away the most in franchise history. Jim Lefebvre was a distant second with 233 wins.

But one thing Lou did not have in '02 that he had had throughout his tenure was right fielder Jay Buhner, the best team leader the franchise ever had. Whereas Ken Griffey Jr. was the grace of the franchise from 1989 through 1998, Jay Buhner was the grunge during his fourteen seasons with the Mariners.

The oft-injured Buhner retired at the end of the 2001 season, one small step from his ultimate goal—playing and winning a World Series.

"Bone," as he was known, kept everyone in the clubhouse in line. You didn't mess with Lou or anyone, or you would hear it from Bone. He was big, bald, and powerful. He also was a clubhouse character, one time emerging from a shower in spring training wearing nothing but a smile and a bagel—in a certain area of his body. Jay took gruff from no one. He spoke, and teammates listened.

Look up the word *competitor,* and you might find a picture of Jay Buhner. There was the time in 1990 when Jim Lefebvre was the manager. The skipper kept lobbying the front office for a right-handed batter with power. Buhner was that guy and was not shy about expressing his opinion.

The proverbial shit hit the fan in a game at the Kingdome when Lefebvre pinch-hit for Buhner. Bone took his bat, walked out the dugout toward the locker room, and proceeded to bash the wall separating him from the dugout. Bang! Bang! Bang! It was so loud you could hear it in the press box.

That wall prevented some serious damage to the manager. The two combatants have remained enemies ever since.

Near the end of camp, I invited Becky to join me in Portland for the final exhibition game of spring training, and we could ride back to Seattle together. She accepted the invitation and took a train to Portland, visiting a longtime friend in the Rose City before I arrived.

The highlight of Becky's trip, I believe, was meeting Dave Niehaus, the Mariners' iconic broadcaster who, in 2009, would be inducted into the National Baseball Hall of Fame in Cooperstown, New York.

David, as I called him, was in his "My, oh, my!" moments early in the regular season as the Mariners went on an eleven-game winning streak in April. It was shades of 2001 all over again as the team won with regularity.

A 15–2 whipping of the Blue Jays on May 16 in Toronto improved the Mariners' record to 28–12. Closer Kaz Sasaki had nine saves en route to a team-leading thirty-seven, and Safeco Field was filled almost every game.

The Mariners ended July with a three-game winning streak and started August with a three-game winning streak. The reigning division champions led the AL West at the end of April, May, June, and July. But August was the month of money ball in Oakland.

The Athletics rattled off an amazing twenty-game winning streak between August 13 and September 4, overtaking the Anaheim Angels, who had been second virtually the entire season, and then the Mariners, who lost six straight from September 9 to 14.

When the dust settled on the season, Oakland won the West with a 103–59 record, Anaheim was four games back with a 99–63 mark, and Seattle finished with a respectable 93–69 record.

The Oakland streak led to the best-selling book *Moneyball*. A movie of the same name starring Brad Pitt as general manager Billy Beane was released to rave reviews in 2011.

If a movie had been made about the Mariners' season, it could have been called *Foolish*.

That's the way third-year CEO Howard Lincoln reacted to an innocuous comment manager Lou Piniella made to a Houston reporter during an interleague series against the Astros in June.

Piniella was asked about the importance of contending teams making personnel moves prior to the July 31 trade deadline. It was Lou's belief that organizations that were active at the deadline improved their playoff chances. Lincoln, who misinterpreted the comment, summoned his manager into his office for a meeting and read him the riot act.

Lincoln's disrespect was crucial to Piniella's departure, but the declining health of Lou's father, Louis, in Tampa, Florida, also was a factor. If I know Lou the way I think I do, he would have finished out his contract with the Mariners if it had not been for Lincoln's misstep. As it was, Louis passed away in 2005, when Lou was managing the hometown Rays.

I doubt that anyone in Seattle took Piniella's departure harder than Bob Finnigan.

He traveled to Tampa for one last story with Lou. Finnie's final self-serving paragraph read something like this: "Well, Finnie, we went through a lot together, didn't we?"

The paragraph never made it into print but gave the *Seattle Times* sports department an opportunity for a group head shake.

More importantly, my relationship with Becky Marsh was blossoming into something fantastic.

Chapter 27

2003: Melvin Moves into Manager's Office

The departure of Lou Piniella, the most popular and successful manager in franchise history, was felt throughout the Pacific Northwest. Mariners fans were disappointed that Lou would not be back in 2003, but he left what everyone thought was a quality team—one that now included outfielder Randy Winn.

In a move that reminded me of the Athletics in 1974, when owner Charlie Finley demanded compensation from the Yankees for Dick Williams, who also resigned as manager with one year remaining on his contract, the Mariners received Winn in a trade with the Devil Rays.

A little more than a month after Piniella walked out of the home team's managerial office at Safeco Field for the last time, a virtual unknown was hired to fill the huge shoes of Sweet Lou. Former big-league catcher and then Arizona Diamondbacks bench coach Bob Melvin was selected as the twelfth skipper in Mariners history over more seasoned skippers Jim Riggleman and Buddy Bell.

"This guy's a good communicator, and I think that's very important at this level," General Manager Pat Gillick said. "Communication and motivation over 162 games is what's really important, and we feel this guy's a strong communicator."

Melvin lacked the experience and name recognition Piniella had had when he was hired ten years earlier.

"I don't have a clue," outfielder Mike Cameron said, referring to the new manager. "From what I've heard, he's a pretty good dude, but other than that, I won't have the slightest idea until I show up for spring training."

Camp opened a little earlier than usual, because the team was supposed to travel to Tokyo to begin the regular season on March 25 against the Athletics in a two-game series. I couldn't think of a better way to celebrate my fifty-eighth birthday.

More importantly, the trip would allow Japanese baseball fans an opportunity to watch Japan products Ichiro, Kazuhiro Sasaki, and Shigetoshi Hasegawa up close once again.

As the March 19 departure date came closer, there were rumors of an imminent attack by the United States against Iraq. Using the alleged presence of weapons of mass destruction as the reason for using force, President George W. Bush, a former Texas Rangers owner, decided that March 19 would be the date of his attack to remove Saddam Hussein from power.

Our bags were packed, and we were ready to board the busses taking us to Sky Harbor Airport when the trip was cancelled by commissioner Bud Selig. We were told that MLB was concerned about the flight from Phoenix to Tokyo. That made little sense to me, considering we would not be flying anywhere close to Iraq, but who was I to question the decision?

"A month ago, everyone knew we were probably going to war," second baseman Bret Boone said, "but until the president comes on and is pretty firm about what's going to happen, it hits home that he isn't messing around. Players watching last night were probably going, 'Wow!' I know I was and realized the trip to Japan was in jeopardy."

As a souvenir of the trip, I kept my boarding pass (row 49) and had it framed.

The Mariners remained in Peoria and opened the season in Oakland against a team coming off that remarkable twenty-game winning streak the previous season. The defending division champs won the first two games of the three-game series before the Mariners made Melvin a winning big-league manager for the first time in the series finale.

The road-weary team returned to Seattle on April 6 following an 11–2 pounding of the Rangers. It was the first time since February 9 that any Mariner had set foot inside Safeco Field.

It also marked the first time I set foot in the house on Forty-First Street in Seattle.

During my first two seasons on the Mariners beat for MLB.com, I stayed with Jeff Melnyk, the son of longtime friend Bob Melnyk, in Enumclaw. On a good day, it was a forty-five-minute drive from his house to Safeco Field, and on bad days it could take well over one hour.

My relationship with Becky was on solid footing, and we thought about me moving into the house where she; her dad, Gene Richardson; her son, Brad; the family dog, Winston; and a pet rabbit named Buster were living. One more would not make a crowd, so my commute was chopped way down, and my relationship with Becky, the most selfless person I had ever met, grew even more.

On the field, the Mariners were sizzling as well. A 20–5 record from May 11 through June 8 boosted their record to 42–19 and gave them an eight-game lead over the Athletics in what many regarded as the toughest division in the major leagues.

But half of that lead was gone by the All-Star break. A six-game skid from August 20 to 25 coupled with a hot streak by the Athletics erased all of the Mariners' division lead.

The Athletics took over sole possession of first place on August 27 and never relinquished their division lead. Even so, the Mariners were still in the hunt for the AL wildcard playoff berth.

Any chance that the Mariners would reach the playoffs ended on September 24 in Anaheim.

Three games involving AL playoff contenders went into extra innings. Two of the contending teams won, but the Mariners weren't one of them.

In Boston, the Red Sox were down to their last strike in the ninth inning when they got a three-run home run and eventual ten-inning victory over the Orioles, strengthening their hold on the wildcard. In Oakland, the Athletics were down to their last strike in the ninth inning when they tied the game and also won in the tenth inning, clinching at least a tie for the AL West championship.

And less than an hour later, at Edison Field, Tim Salmon hit a one-out home run off Shigetoshi Hasegawa in the eleventh inning, giving the Angels a 2–1 win that handed the Athletics their second straight division title.

The Red Sox clinched the AL wildcard berth the following night. The Mariners finished the season with a 93–69 record, matching the second-highest win total in a single season—something they also had accomplished the previous season.

Left-hander Jamie Moyer won a career-best twenty-one games, and for the first time since the Dodgers in 1966, the Mariners used just five starting pitchers the entire season—Moyer, Freddy Garcia, Joel Pineiro, Ryan Franklin, and Gil Meche. Second baseman Bret Boone led the team with thirty-five home runs, while Ichiro reached the two-hundred-hit plateau for the third consecutive season.

General Manager Pat Gillick announced after the season that he was retiring but remained with the organization on a consulting basis. A franchise that had enjoyed its heyday—from Lou Piniella's arrival prior to the '93 season to Gillick's departure—was on the verge of falling off the face of the MLB playoff-contending landscape.

My life, though, was looking up.

Becky and I decided to take a Hawaii vacation, and upon our arrival in Kona, Hawaii, I proposed. She accepted.

Chapter 28

2004: Why the Long Face?

The Mariners had two in-house general manager candidates to take over where Pat Gillick left off. But neither Benny Looper nor Lee Pelekoudas got the job. It went to an outsider, forty-five-year-old Bill Bavasi.

All I knew about him was that he was the son of former MLB executive Buzzie Bavasi and was running the show for the Angels during that team's memorable collapse in 1995 when the Mariners overcame a thirteen-game deficit in August and captured their first AL West championship.

Perhaps hiring Bavasi as the new general manager was the Mariners' way of saying thank you for the job he did in Anaheim to allow one of the greatest comebacks in MLB history to happen.

I would soon learn that honesty was not one of Bavasi's strong suits. Nor were trading for players or signing free agents. He was, without a doubt, the worst general manager in franchise history, and the organization is still reeling from the countless mistakes he made.

Rather than going into his many blunders here, I'll just suggest that you read his bio on Wikipedia if you're interested.

The annual winter meetings in 2003 were held in New Orleans, and Bavasi zeroed in on free-agent shortstop Miguel Tejada, the AL MVP in 2002 with the Athletics. Gillick had gone to Tejada's off-season home to measure the player's interest in the Mariners.

Tejada was interested in signing a multiyear deal, but the Mariners weren't the only team pursuing him. Seattle, flush with cash following another year of 3 million-plus home attendance, offered Miguel a four-year deal that would have made him the highest-paid player in franchise history.

Tejada's agent rejected the offer, telling the Mariners that his client had a better offer from another organization. The Mariners stuck to their four-year deal, and Tejada accepted a five-year offer from the Baltimore Orioles.

According to a story in the *Seattle Times* written by Larry Stone, the newspaper's national baseball writer, the Mariners turned their attention to the Indians, offering Carlos Guillen for Omar Vizquel.

A long list of injuries and a DUI charge had soured the Mariners on Guillen, a switch-hitter. Vizquel, also a switch-hitter, had excelled for the Mariners in the early 1990s before being dealt to Cleveland to make room for Alex Rodriguez. Omar was ready, willing, and able to return to Seattle.

I called Bavasi to ask about Stone's report, and the new general manager denied it, saying he had no interest in Vizquel and had not even talked to the Indians in several weeks.

Something told me to check it out, so I called Paul Hoynes, the Indians beat reporter for the *Cleveland Plain Dealer,* and asked if he had Omar's home phone number.

He did. I called. Omar answered.

"They called me about an hour ago and told me I didn't pass the test on my knee," Vizquel said from his Issaquah, Washington, home. "It was kind of a shock. I was really looking forward to coming back and playing for the Mariners."

The knee injury limited Omar to sixty-four games in 2003, but he was certain that he was near 100 percent health when he went through a workout at Safeco Field.

"I don't know who made the final decision, but I guess they didn't like what they saw," the thirty-six-year-old said. "I did a bunch of tests, and they moved my knee up and down. I have been working out every day, and my knee is feeling good—it's getting there. I was really surprised that I didn't pass. I look strong, you know."

Bavasi would not return my phone calls.

Omar played in 148 games for the Indians in 2004, batting .291 with seven home runs and fi fty-seven RBIs, and has a good chance of being inducted into the National Baseball Hall of Fame the fi rst time he is on the ballot.

Bavasi eventually traded Guillen to the Tigers for infielder Ramon Santiago, who played in eighteen games. Rich Aurelia handled the shortstop duties for seventy-three games, batting .241 with four home runs and twenty-eight RBIs. Jose Lopez, a rookie, also played some shortstop, but the position was basically a disaster from the get-go.

Not so with second base.

For the fourth consecutive season, spring training opened with Bret Boone manning the position with flair and production. He was funny, entertaining, talented, and the undisputed team leader in the clubhouse. He was known as "the Boone." And who came up with the name? He did.

Bret got along great with the writers, informing all of us that if it weren't for him, we would all be out of jobs. Of course, we said that if it weren't for us, no one ever would have heard of him. To get our point across, I arranged to have t-shirts made and worn by the scribes at a morning spring-training practice.

About ten of us put on the dark-blue shirts with white lettering: "We Made the Boone."

The team made a mess of the regular season, losing eight of their first ten games. A six-game losing streak the first week of May knocked the team far below .500. It would never come close to the break-even mark, finishing the woeful season with ninety-nine losses and last in the AL West.

Besides screwing up the shortstop position, Bavasi bungled big-time by signing Scott Spiezio to a three-year, $9 million contract. Spiezio batted .215 in 2004 and played only twenty-nine games the following season, batting .064 (three for forty-seven) before the Mariners released him on August 19, 2005, not a moment too soon.

The '04 season was memorable for two reasons, not at all in this order: Ichiro set a major-league single-season hit record with 262, breaking an eighty-two-year-old record, and Becky Marsh became Becky Street on May 1.

On the field, Ichiro made it four straight two-hundred-plus seasons and was a complete jerk about it. He would rarely give local beat writers the time of day, let alone decent answers to good questions. He was especially rude to John Hickey, the *Seattle Post-Intelligencer* reporter. John is overweight, and Ichiro would make fun of Hickey's physique, speaking only in Japanese, leaving it up to his interpreter to embarrass the veteran baseball writer.

I asked John why he didn't tell Ichiro where to go. Hickey was getting a nice income from the Japanese publications for the stories he wrote involving the Mariners' Japanese players—especially Ichiro. Don't bite the hand that feeds you.

Off the field, Becky and I decided to get married at the end of the baseball season at the home of one our friends. But that was not working out as well as we had hoped, so we decided to elope. We would get married in Las Vegas, Nevada, on May Day and have our families travel to Seattle for a two-day celebration at the end of the season. After all, this was not the first rodeo for either of us when it came to marriage vows.

I made a huge blunder by not telling my kids until after the fact. My reasoning: the chapel was small and was limited to the amount of guests who could attend. My older brother and his wife were invited, along with Becky's dad, Gene. My parents drove from Dorris to 'Vegas to surprise us, and we managed to get everyone seats in the Little Chapel of the Flowers.

My daughter, Katy, did not take the news well and still has not forgotten or forgiven. My son, Scott, thankfully moved past my blunder. It was never an issue with Becky's son, Brad.

Speaking of blunders, Bavasi had one final surprise up his sleeve in the '04 season. He fired Melvin.

It had become clear near the end of the season that Melvin was on his way out. For starters, Bavasi stopped communicating with his manager, so it wasn't a big surprise when Melvin received word that he was being replaced.

A few days before the axe fell, the team was in Arlington, Texas, for a series against the Rangers. As I walked through the door into the visiting manager's office before the game, Bob Finnigan was walking out the door.

I walked in and saw Melvin brandishing the biggest middle finger I'd ever seen, obviously aimed at Finnigan.

I couldn't have said it any better.

All that remained was a similar gesture to Bavasi.

"I think this is not to lay the blame for the number of losses right at Bob's doorstop," Bavasi said. "That's not our intention. I've absolutely nothing negative to say about Bob. He's a real good man, he worked hard, cared about his players. But to go forward, we thought a change was in order."

In almost the same breath, Bavasi said he would recommend Melvin to the Arizona Diamondbacks, who had fired Bob Brenly three years after he managed the Diamondbacks to the World Series. Melvin got the job, earned National League Manager of the Year honors in 2007, and was selected as the AL Manager of the Year in 2012 with the Oakland Athletics, becoming the fifth manager in MLB history to earn Manager of the Year in both leagues.

The Mariners haven't had a Manager of the Year since Lou Piniella in 2001.

There would, however, be many more ways Bill Bavasi would single-handedly dismantle the franchise and drive thousands of Mariners fans away from the ballpark. Amazingly, the front office let him get away with it.

On a brighter note, my season ended in late October in St. Louis. I was selected by the MLB.com execs in New York City to be on the team of reporters covering the World Series between the Red Sox and Cardinals. The AL champion Bosox made quick work of the Redbirds, sweeping the series in four games. It was Boston's first World Series championship in eighty-six years.

I actually watched the Fall Classic on television, as my seat assignments were in the Fenway Park media dining room and the hallway outside the Cardinals clubhouse at Busch Stadium. John Ralph, the central region editor, was the engine that drove the MLB.com machine and one of the most professional editors I had the pleasure of working with in my forty-year sportswriting career.

It was the twelfth time—and the last time—that I covered a World Series.

Two weeks after the season, Becky and I went on a one-week honeymoon to the Hyatt El Dorado Resort in Puerto Rico. We played golf the first day and dodge-the-rain-drops during the remaining six days of our visit.

Chapter 29

2005: A Big Splash in the Free-Agent Market

I was on my way from the clubhouse level to the press box at Safeco Field during the second day of the annual two-day FanFest when the elevator door opened and there stood General Manager Bill Bavasi and free-agent pitcher Jeff Nelson.

"Is there something going on that I should know about?" I asked.

"No," Bavasi answered. "We're just visiting. Nothing is going on."

I went to the press box and called Nelson's home. His wife, Collette, answered, and I asked her if there was any chance of her husband returning to the Mariners. She said Jeff and the team already had reached agreement on a minor-league contract that included an invitation to spring training.

It didn't surprise me that Bavasi had told me something totally different. It wasn't the first time it happened and wouldn't be the last.

Nellie spent the first four years of his major-league career with Seattle (1992–1995) before being traded to the Yankees. He returned to the Mariners prior to the 2001 season and departed again midway through the '03 campaign, soon after criticizing club officials for not making personnel moves prior to the July 31 trading deadline.

Nelson apologized the following day, but within a week he was dealt back to the Yankees for right-handed reliever Armando Benitez.

"I was wrong in what I said. I didn't mean it the way it came out," Nellie said after his signing became official. "Everybody gets in arguments with their family. A lot of times things are said out of context and you later regret saying them.

"I consider [the Mariners] part of my family, and the whole situation has bothered me. Everything that happened in 2003 has been weighing on my mind, and I was able to talk to Chuck [club president Chuck Armstrong] today. I also want to talk to Howard [CEO Howard Lincoln]. I know there has been a strain in the relationship, and I want to mend fences."

The Mariners family in 2005 included a new manager, Mike Hargrove, and a pair of middle-of-the-lineup sluggers—third baseman Adrian Beltre and first baseman Richie Sexson. They had been signed for a whopping $114 million the previous December.

Beltre, coming off a career year with the Dodgers, was lured to Seattle with a five-year, $64 million contract. The Mariners outbid the Orioles for Sexson, bringing the northwest native back home with a four-year, $50 million deal.

Sexson hit home runs in his first two regular-season at bats against the Twins at Safeco Field. The Mariners entered May with a 12–12 record but went on a seven-game losing streak, triggering another ninety-plus-loss season.

A two-time All-Star selection with the Brewers (2002 and 2003), Sexson had a hit-and-miss first season for the Mariners. He led the team with thirty-nine home runs and 121 RBIs. He led the league with 167 strikeouts.

But by Bavasi standards, this was a good start for one of his major investments.

Not so with Beltre.

The classy third baseman tried his best to warrant the huge contract he had received. For whatever reason, including the fact Safeco Field was not friendly to right-handed sluggers, Beltre's batting average went from .334 in '04 to .255 in '05; his home run total tumbled from forty-eight to nineteen; and his RBIs dropped from 121 to 87.

To his credit, Beltre never complained about the ballpark. He continued to grind away, and although he would never admit it, I felt that his contract and the unfairness of pitcher-friendly Safeco Field bothered him.

Beltre was the antithesis of Bret Boone. Whereas most of Beltre's power was to left and left center, places where potential home runs go to die, Boonie had a knack for hitting the ball with power the other way—to right field, where it was much easier to reach the seats, even for a right-handed batter. The ballpark was, after all, built to take full advantage of Ken Griffey Jr.'s power.

It was a graveyard for the likes of Beltre and other right-handed hitters, such as Mike Cameron and Jeff Cirillo. Safeco Field was their kryptonite.

"I'm a big part of the failure of this team," Beltre said.

It became obvious early in May that the Mariners would not be returning to the playoffs. As June turned to July, the writing also was on the wall that Boone was on his way out. He was designated for assignment on July 3 and conducted one of the most heart-wrenching press conferences I had ever attended.

Boone choked up several times during the session.

"It's a pretty sad day for me," he said.

It was a pretty sad day for the media as well. Boone had been the go-to guy before and after games, win or lose. He was a standup guy if there ever was one. He was funny and could mimic every reporter covering the team and had two lockers at Safeco, both of them filled with bats. Boone must have had about a hundred bats at any given time. His locker looked like a lumber factory.

He often called the reporters clowns. The reporters knew Boonie was a bigger clown than any of us, and he liked that. Tit-for-tat was okay with the Boone.

The Mariners eventually traded Bret to the Twins for cash and a player that would never set foot in Safeco Field.

At the time, I had other things on my mind—specifically my daughter's wedding in mid-August. She had met her future husband at a Padres game in San Diego. (I had arranged for her and her mom to get tickets.)

The parents established a wedding budget.

A few weeks before the wedding, I received a phone call from a sobbing daughter telling me that she had had a fight with her mom. During the conversation, she said her mom had told her that she would not pay her share of the wedding. Her mind could not be changed. As a result, the money Becky and I had put aside for a Hawaiian vacation at the end of the baseball season suddenly became earmarked for the wedding.

Even, so, one of the proudest moments of my life came when Katy and I danced to Bette Midler's "Wind Beneath My Wings" at the wedding.

The season ended with ninety-three losses and another last-place finish in the AL West.

Instead of going on vacation to Hawaii, Becky and I drove to Tucson, where her father had spent the summer watching over the house on North Divot Drive.

In the meantime, I had asked John Schlegel, my immediate supervisor, if it would be possible to leave the Mariners beat and work out of my Tucson house. Dinn Mann at MLB.com headquarters approved the move, and I attended the winter meetings in December as a national reporter.

Chapter 30

2006: A Year in the Desert

After leaving the Mariners beat, I expected my career with MLB.com to last at least five more years as a national reporter. I figured it would reduce the amount of travel I was doing—about fifty thousand miles a season—and give me more time at home with my wife.

Late in the 2005 season, John Schlegel, the west region editor, asked me to give him my recommendation for who would replace me on the Mariners beat. I said either Bob Sherwin or Kirby Arnold would do a great job, as both were veteran writers and knew the team and organization extremely well.

Bob was doing some freelance work after getting royally screwed at the *Seattle Times,* where he was professionally humiliated by sports editor Cathy Henkel. Kirby covered the Mariners like a blanket for the *Everett Herald* and had become a good friend following my return to the beat in 2001. He was a terrific writer and beat me like a drum at golf. But I didn't hold that against him.

Schlegel thanked me for my suggestion—and hired Corey Brock, the backup baseball writer at the *Tacoma News-Tribune.* At the time, I was disappointed that neither of my recommendations was selected. Within a year, I was extremely happy Corey got the gig.

Although MLB.com initially was regarded throughout the newspaper industry as an extension of the teams' public-relations departments, that was far from accurate. Dinn Mann hired seasoned baseball writers like Ken Gurnick (Dodgers), Carrie Muskat (Cubs), Tom Singer (Angels),

Rich Draper (Diamondbacks), Chris Haft (Reds), and John Schlegel (Padres), giving the organization instant credibility, and later added the likes of T.R. Sullivan (Rangers).

MLB.com became a supersuccessful start-up company, and it was cool to be a part of the company's growth. We worked just as hard, if not harder, than most beat reporters and were rewarded for it via annual bonuses and raises—two words that had become obsolete in the newspaper industry.

Furthermore, MLB.com invited all of its reporters and New York–based employees to a Christmas party each year in the Big Apple, picking up the tab for flight and hotel accommodations. The hotel rooms were pretty awful, but turning out the lights worked wonders.

The first World Baseball Classic was set for the spring of '06, and I volunteered my services for the games being played in Tokyo. I was well acquainted with Ichiro, who was going to play for Japan, and the team representing China was managed by Jim Lefebvre, whom I had known for many years. The China team would be preparing for the Classic in Scottsdale, Arizona, a short drive from our house in Tucson.

I was assigned to cover the Classic in Japan.

One of the first e-mails I sent out was to Susumu Fukatsu, my friend and tour guide when I was in Japan in 1969. We were supposed to meet up and have dinner when the Mariners traveled to Japan in 2003, but that plan was nixed when the US attacked Iraq. As a result, I had not seen Susumu since '69. We quickly reconnected on the information highway and made dinner plans for the night after I arrived in Tokyo. He wanted me to meet his wife and daughter.

Susumu had become a successful businessman selling plastic products in Asia. He had clients in Hanoi, Vietnam, of all places.

The trip to Japan went just as I had expected. The dinner with Susumu and his family was a lot of fun, and the World Baseball Classic games were a combination of blowouts—usually involving the overmatched team from China—and nail-biters. Team Japan and South Korea met in the final game, with the Koreans winning 3–2. Both advanced to the second round, which was played in Anaheim.

During the workout day before the first game, Bob Sherwin and I asked for an interview with Japan manager Sadaharu Oh. He obliged, and we talked about such things as why Ichiro had not taken more of a leadership role with the Mariners.

Oh, the sport's all-time home run leader, explained that it wasn't in the DNA of an Asian player to be a leader on a team from another country. But the most interesting part of the interview was how the Japanese media standing around the area behind home plate surrounded Sherwin and me as we interviewed the legendary Oh. It was almost like they were afraid to approach him and ask questions.

I helped with the coverage for the games played in Anaheim and also the final round in San Diego, where Japan defeated Cuba for the first Classic championship. It was one of the best experiences of my career and one I will always remember.

Following the Classic, I settled into my new job with MLB.com, primarily writing stories from my home office. My stress level subsided substantially as I worked on such things as "Peek at the Week," MLB.com's first power rankings, the "Fab 15," and "Day at the Races." I also covered some games, filling in for beat reporters on their days off.

When the Mariners played a three-game interleague series against the Diamondbacks in Phoenix, I was assigned to cover the Mariners. The series was in late June, and one of the stories I was assigned to write was an update on the All-Star voting.

Ichiro was the only Mariners player listed among the leading vote getters, and I needed to get a quote from him. I arrived at the ballpark and asked Ichiro's translator, Ken Barron, if I could get a few seconds with Ichiro to ask him one question.

Barron talked to Ichiro (in Japanese) and came back to me, saying Ichiro would meet me in the clubhouse after his pregame batting practice. I followed the right fielder into the clubhouse and waited for him to acknowledge me. With Barron standing nearby, Ichiro turned his back on me and let out the loudest fart I can remember hearing.

They laughed. I didn't.

I walked out of the clubhouse and later filed my sidebar—without a quote from his highness.

Going forward, it will give me great pleasure to omit his name from the Hall of Fame ballot I'll fill in five years after his retirement. There is more to being a Hall of Famer than the number of hits you get during a career. He should be in the Hall of Shame, not the Hall of Fame.

From the day Ichiro arrived from Japan to the day I retired, he was exceedingly rude to American reporters, whether giving snide answers to good questions or making fun of Hickey's girth. I had one Japanese reporter tell me, "If you think he's rude to you guys, he treats us even worse."

For the most part, Ichiro would talk to one or two Japan-based reporters after games, and those reporters would share the quotes with the other reporters.

The second half of the season went much better, and I was assigned to be on the MLB.com team that covered the Mets-Dodgers playoff series.

Near the end of the calendar year, I received a phone call from Schlegel. He told me that the reporter covering the Angels was getting off the beat, the Padres reporter was going to cover the Angels, and there was a good chance that my national reporter job was going to be eliminated.

That was not real good news.

John gave me some options: I could become the Padres beat reporter and move to San Diego; I could cover beach volleyball in Huntington Beach; or, if I could get Corey Brock to move to San Diego and cover the Padres, I could return to Seattle and cover the Mariners.

Bless his big heart, Corey moved to San Diego, and it was back on the Mariners beat for me. Luckily for me, it was Corey who had replaced me prior to the '06 season. If it had been either Kirby or Bob, I probably would have been involved in the first and only layoff in MLB. com history, occurring shortly before the winter meetings.

Becky was never keen on Tucson (too hot for her) and was thrilled beyond words to return to the Northwest. She is a top-of-the-line interior designer and could not find enough top-of-the-line clients in Tucson to keep her busy.

Our house, which she completely remodeled, became our vacation villa.

The Mariners, meanwhile, finished last in the AL West despite winning seventy-eight games. It was their third consecutive last-place finish. General Manager Bill Bavasi was on a roll.

Chapter 31

2007: A Journey to South America

Among the benefits of traveling more than fifty thousand miles and spending about a hundred nights a year in hotel rooms are the award points you can accumulate.

Thanks to United and Continental Airlines, along with Hyatt, Westin, and Marriott Hotels, I was able to pile up enough miles over the years to visit places in the world I otherwise never would have been able to see.

It was with some of those points I was able to send my parents to Nashville, Tennessee, for their 50th wedding anniversary, my son to Paris as a graduation gift from college (UCLA), and my daughter to Florida and Hawaii.

It was our turn in 2006, as Becky and I spent a couple of weeks in South America, first in Rio de Janeiro and then in Buenos Aires. Unlike on many of our other vacations, inclement weather was not a factor. We had a blast in both countries and assembled enough memories to last a lifetime.

We returned to Tucson on the Tuesday before Thanksgiving. Awaiting me on my computer was an assignment from MLB.com—write a story on the Japanese players most likely to play in the major leagues in 2007. The deadline: the next day.

Once the panic subsided, I made a few phone calls. None of them were answered. It was the day before Thanksgiving, and offices were closed. I finally got in touch via phone with Jim Marshall, a longtime friend and Pacific Rim scout for the Arizona Diamondbacks. He gave me some names of players, along with the name of another scout.

Fortunately, I was able to meet the story deadline, and the nerves finally settled down.

I actually was excited about returning to the Mariners beat—even if Bill Bavasi was still the general manager. The year away from the daily grind had recharged my battery, and Becky was much happier to be back in her rainy environment.

The house she made a home in Tucson would have to serve as a summer home for her dad, Gene, and a winter home for me. She would come to Tucson for a week at a time every other month during the winter.

Spring training opened in February, and there was something different. Bob Finnigan no longer was covering the team for the *Seattle Times*. He was replaced by Geoff Baker, a transplanted Canadian who introduced the words *me, myself,* and *I* to journalism.

Whereas Finnie was an extension of the Mariners' public-relations department in print, Baker was just the opposite. He was critical of the players and management. It sometimes bordered on mean-spirited. But the subject he enjoyed writing about the most was Geoff Baker.

Baker unveiled the *Geoff Baker Live! Show* during spring training. He would set up his "studio" outside the door of the media room at the Peoria Sports Complex and communicate with his fans. It was something we seasoned (old) scribes never had seen before.

Larry LaRue (also known as "Lash") of the *Tacoma News-Tribune* came up with a great idea: purchase a pair of funny nose glasses, put them on, and sneak up behind Baker during his show. It was a brilliant idea. Kirby Arnold of the *Everett Herald* and I were coconspirators.

And so, midway through camp, Lash brought the glasses to camp, and we took turns interrupting *Geoff Baker Live!* Geoff actually was a good sport about it, and we all had a good laugh.

Between the video, blogging, tweeting, and writing, Baker was the busiest writer on the beat. I figured he would burn out before the regular-season opener. But writing about himself seemed to keep the adrenaline flowing. When he wasn't blogging, tweeting, or otherwise pontificating about himself, he was chatting about all of the places in the world he had visited in his life.

I figured he must have piled up a bunch of air miles in his young career.

He was the antithesis of his predecessor, and that was good as far as I was concerned. Whereas Finnie would rip players behind their backs upstairs in the press box and kiss their butts downstairs in the clubhouse, Baker ripped them upstairs and downstairs.

The Mariners broke camp with a so-so starting rotation and a bullpen anchored by dependable right-handed closer J. J. Putz. The offense was improved greatly with the signing of free agent Jose Guillen, a problem child when he played for the Angels but a productive bat the Mariners needed.

Felix Hernandez pitched Seattle to a shutout victory over the Athletics in the season opener at Safeco Field, and the Mariners made it two straight the following night before losing the series finale.

Then it was off to Cleveland for a four-game series to kick off a seven-game road trip.

Snow flurries caused the series opener to be delayed four times. With the Indians leading 4–0 in the top of the fifth inning and the Mariners down to their last strike to make the game official, second baseman Jose Lopez repeatedly stepped out of the batter's box and complained to the plate umpire that he couldn't see the ball through all the falling snow.

Lopez said he actually told plate umpire Alfonso Marquez twice that he couldn't see the ball.

"He told me, 'One more pitch,'" Lopez said. "I got lucky and fouled it off, but then I turned to skip [manager Mike Hargrove] and motioned that I couldn't see."

Known as the human rain delay when he played for the Indians, Hargrove sauntered out of the visiting dugout and eventually convinced the umpiring crew to stop the game.

The game finally was canceled after a seventy-seven-minute snow delay. The Mariners had no hits, but it didn't matter. Everything that happened in the game was wiped out.

It snowed all night. It snowed the next day, the day after that, and one more day. All four games in the four-game series were snowed out and rescheduled for May 21, June 11, August 30, and September 26. Those days were supposed to be off days for the Mariners.

The Mariners played well early in the season, especially in May and June, when a MLB-best 25–12 record from May 22 to June 30 had them in second place in the AL West, four games behind the Angels with a 44–33 record.

Every die-hard Mariners fan circled June 22–24 on his or her calendar. It was a three-game interleague series against the Cincinnati Reds at Safeco Field.

Ken Griffey Jr. would be coming home.

Junior refused to discuss with the media his return to Safeco Field. Perhaps he was worried that the reception would be similar to what Alex Rodriguez had in 2001 with the Texas Rangers.

A-Rod was absolutely vilified by Mariners fans when the Rangers played the Mariners in early April that year. Many fans tossed Monopoly money from the stands. One guy, standing near the visiting dugout, brought a fishing pole to the park and attached a real bill to the hook. He cast the line in A-Rod's direction and barely missed the target. It was so bad that Rangers owner Tom Hicks called Mariners president Chuck Armstrong to complain about the treatment Rodriquez received.

Griffey had to be well aware of the treatment his former teammate had received.

But the three-game series against the Reds was a love fest. Junior was still loved in Seattle.

All three games sold out, matching the previous season total. The Reds won the series two games to one, but Mariners fans were the big winners.

"It was everything I thought it would be and more," Griffey said. "It was nice to be back, nice to see some friends and family that I haven't seen in a while. I really enjoyed my time here, the four days I was here. I always thought I would be back. I just never knew when."

I received a phone call at our home late on the morning of July 1.

The Mariners were having a press conference at Safeco Field. What could it be? The team was on an eight-game winning streak, so perhaps Hargrove was receiving a contract extension. Heck, maybe Bill Bavasi was getting a lifetime contract extension from the organization. That thought made my stomach hurt.

I wasn't prepared for this bombshell.

Hargrove was stepping down as the manager, saying he no longer could give the same passion or commitment to his bosses and players. Bench coach John McLaren was named as Hargrove's replacement. The Mariners had won eight consecutive games between June 23 and July 1, making Hargrove the first manager since 1900 to resign his position after a winning streak of more than seven games.

McLaren, who had a longtime desire to manage in the major leagues, preferably the Mariners, was among those stunned by the news. He recently had undergone shoulder surgery and was still in a sling.

"This is not the perfect scenario for taking over a ball club, but Mike gave me his blessing, and that meant a lot," McLaren said. "I have waited for this day, and my emotions are running high. I feel confident, and I'll be ready to go."

It was one of the weirdest days of my career. I mean a manager just doesn't walk away from his job, especially when the team is playing as well as the Mariners were at the time. Rumors suggested that Ichiro had gone to upper management and said he wouldn't sign a contract extension at the end of the season if Hargrove was the manager. That made perfect sense, but I could never get the rumor confirmed.

The passion Hargrove didn't have in '07 apparently returned a few years later when he was a strong candidate to fill the Indians' managerial position but lost out to Manny Acta. Hargrove was so confident that he'd get the job he began assembling a coaching staff.

His bench coach might have been Ron Hassey. The former MLB catcher was Hargrove's bench coach with the Mariners before Hassey surprisingly was fired. I am not sure if it had anything to do with his dismissal, but when the team was in Boston for a series, Hassey had the audacity to move the batting gloves sitting on the bench.

The gloves belonged to Ichiro, who had a daily routine of putting two bats and his batting gloves in a particular place in the dugout prior to pregame conditioning drills in the outfield. No one dared touch Ichiro's property. The Mariners remained in the playoff hunt until early

September, when a season-high nine-game losing streak knocked them for a collective loop. Even so, the team finished with an 88–74 record, finishing second in the AL West.

Bavasi kept his job, giving him a little more time to finish his dismantling of the franchise.

Chapter 32

2008: A Devastating Trade with the Orioles

A rejuvenated offense that included six players with at least twenty home runs, a team-leading 105 RBIs from Raul Ibanez, and 99 from Adrian Beltre and Jose Guillen, convinced General Manager Bill Bavasi that the Mariners were two good starting pitchers away from challenging for the AL West title in 2008. It didn't seem to faze the general manager that Guillen, one of the team's clubhouse leaders, was allowed to leave via free agency.

That, it turned out, was a bad decision. But by this time, there were so many bad Bavasi decisions that Mariners fans had stopped counting.

Another bonehead move occurred in December, when Bavasi signed sinker-ball specialist Carlos Silva to a four-year, $46 million contract. The overweight right-hander with barely a .500 career record felt the pressure of the big contract, came unglued several times during the '08 season, and finished with a 4–15 record. He would win one game the following season before being traded to the Cubs for outfielder Milton Bradley.

As horrible as the Silva signing turned out to be, the deal that probably sealed Bavasi's fate with the organization came on February 8, a week or so before spring training opened in Peoria, Arizona. Come hell or high water, Bavasi was determined to acquire Orioles left-hander Erik Bedard, regarded throughout the industry as a five-inning pitcher and as soft as a roll of Charmin bath tissue.

All it cost the franchise was outfielder Adam Jones, the best draft selection the Mariners had made since landing Alex Rodriguez with the number-one overall selection in 1993, and four other players—lefty reliever George Sherrill and minor-league pitchers Chris Tillman, Tony Butler, and Kam Mickileo.

Jones was a budding star, a five-tool player that many, including me, expected to patrol center field for the Mariners the way Ken Griffey Jr. did in the 1990s and Mike Cameron did in the early 2000s.

"My dad always told me, 'Don't trade an everyday player for a pitcher,'" Bavasi said at a February 8 press conference announcing the trade. "I am going against his philosophy."

He should have listened to his dad, although he often referred to him as "Buzzie," something I always considered disrespectful.

"We did give up some good young kids, but we think now it's time to go out and win," The Mariners general manager said. "That's the most significant aspect of this deal. This gives us what we think is a good rotation one through five."

Bavasi declared the rotation of Bedard, Felix Hernandez, Silva, Miguel Batista, and Jarrod Washburn "Maybe as good as there is."

Or maybe not.

The first misstep of spring training possibly came the day before camp opened. Bedard, who avoided salary arbitration by signing a one-year $7 million contract, walked into camp a few minutes after manager John McLaren told the early-arriving beat reporters that Bedard would be the Mariners' opening-day starter. Right-hander Felix Hernandez, the anticipated opening-day starter for the second straight season, who had compiled a 14–7 record, took the news in stride. He could have complained and asked for a chance to at least compete for the opening-day start.

It was, shall we say, surprising to a lot of people.

"It kind of caught me by surprise, coming so early in spring like this," Bedard said. "Being the opening-day starter never was a goal of mine. Felix is the number-one starter here. I don't know why everyone makes such a big deal about it. After that, there isn't much hype."

Bedard led the major leagues in home runs allowed during spring training—nine in twenty-four innings—but the regular season opened with Bedard on the mound pitching against the Rangers at Safeco Field. He surrendered three hits and one run over seven innings.

His second start was scheduled for six days later against the Orioles in Baltimore.

"The first thing that enters your mind when you wake up and don't feel right is that you might not be able to pitch," said Bedard after being scratched from the start because of inflammation in his left hip area. He had no idea how it happened.

As April turned to May, my attention went to Southern California, where my daughter was giving birth to my first grandchild. Avery was born on May 12, the day before Mother's Day.

Meanwhile, a team expected to challenge for a playoff spot struggled from the get-go, and on June 16, with a major-league-worst 24–45 record, Bill Bavasi was fired. Many wondered what took so long.

"We have tried to be patient, some say too patient," CEO Howard Lincoln said. "But given this team's record, change is in order."

Bavasi attended the press conference. "It's really ironic that the person we're missing the most is Jose Guillen," he said. "That is the piece that was here last year is not here this year. He could do some strange things, and he did, but at the top of his agenda was to win, and if anybody got in the way of playing the game right, he had no patience with that. That was his boiling point."

Bavasi said the current clubhouse was filled with "nice guys who think they are trying hard, but someone must step up and be willing to grab a teammate by the collar."

He called the current team dysfunctional and had no clue as to why almost the entire team underperformed so badly.

"I don't have a reason for that," he said. "I think this club on the field can perform a helluva lot better than it is performing now. It has not lost its talent or gotten old all of a sudden. It has learned to be dysfunctional, and they have to unlearn that. They are not playing the game the way they can.

"They should be able to perform better, and they can't look to the manager or coaches to lead them out of this. They have to rescue themselves."

They didn't rescue themselves. The Mariners ended the season with a 61–101 record, becoming the first team in MLB history to lose at least a hundred games with a payroll of at least $100 million. It was not a pretty sight and just might have been the worst season in franchise history.

Baker was at the top of his game, delivering one critical aspect of the season after another. I recall one time, when the team was preparing for pregame workouts at the Oakland Coliseum, Geoff went into a rage while doing one of his many radio shows, and the players overheard him. They were livid, but Baker either didn't notice or didn't care. He kept right on ripping them.

Victims of this shattered season were scattered all over the landscape.

Manager John McLaren and most of his coaching staff were fired. Players that were supposed to lead this team into the postseason for the first time in seven seasons were invited to leave and to take their money owed with them.

The list included Richie Sexson, who was released in early September.

"The time had come when it just didn't seem like it was going to happen here for Richie," said interim manager Jim Riggleman. "I still think he has some baseball left in him, but we weren't able to find the key to open the lock. Maybe it will happen for him somewhere else."

The Mariners were responsible for the remainder of Sexson's four-year $50 million contract, which was slightly more than $7 million.

The media didn't miss him, and he probably didn't miss us. He once told me that the worst part of his job was talking to us. I told him that the worst part of our job was talking to players like him.

"The way I was going to be making up the lineup over the next couple of weeks, we were not going to be able to make Richie happy," Riggleman said. "He has been in the lineup every day until yesterday, and when he wasn't, he was not happy about it. Nothing was said, but his body language indicated that he was a little perturbed by that.

"I thought, *You know what, this is the way it's going to be in the near future,* so rather than have that, I felt it was time to do this. I wish that wasn't the case, but it wasn't going to happen here in the immediate future."

Meanwhile, the Mariners franchise was in dire need of a pick-me-up, and it occurred in October.

Ken Griffey Jr. filed for free agency, opening the door to his possible return to the Mariners.

Griffey made a triumphant return to Seattle during the 2007 season when the Reds visited Safeco Field for an interleague series against the Mariners. Junior hit two home runs in the three games, was cheered wildly every time he came to bat, and said after the series that he missed Seattle more than he ever could have imagined. During a TV interview, Junior said he wanted to end his career where it started.

"Junior has always had a special relationship with the people in Seattle including the fans and people still in the organization," his agent, Brian Goldberg, said, adding that his client would be open-minded about returning to the organization that made him the first overall draft selection in 1987, a selection that helped turn the franchise into a perennial playoff contender in the 1990s.

Griffey, who spent the first eleven seasons of his Hall of Fame career with the Mariners before being traded to the Cincinnati Reds, had an option year remaining on the nine-year contract he had signed with Cincinnati prior to the 2000 season. But the Chicago White Sox, who acquired Junior late in the '08 season, declined the $16.5 million option.

The door was open for the franchise icon to return.

Chapter 33

2009: Who Says You Can't Go Home?

The chatter about Ken Griffey Jr. possibly returning to Seattle to end his Hall of Fame career picked up during the first week of December before the winter meetings held in Las Vegas, Nevada. The odds of Junior coming back to the Mariners initially seemed slim, as second-year General Manager Jack Zduriencik said he wanted to load up his roster with young, athletic players.

The thirty-nine-year-old Griffey fit neither of those criteria.

But all four of the Mariners' Hall of Fame members—Alvin Davis, Jay Buhner, Edgar Martinez, and Dave Niehaus—told me they supported the idea of Junior returning to Seattle.

"Ah, man, that would be great," Davis said from his Riverside, California, home. "I think he still has some gas left in the tank, and now, with Raul [Ibanez] signing with the Phillies, the team really needs a left-handed bat in the heart of the [lineup]. If Junior is healthy, he still is an extremely gifted athlete."

Buhner, who played alongside Griffey in the Mariners outfield from 1989 through 1999, said, "I am being selfish, obviously, but I would love to see him come back. His bat speed isn't what it used to be, nor is his foot speed, but I still think Junior could help the ball club."

Martinez said, "I think it would be great for the team, and the city, to have Junior come back. He belongs in a Mariners uniform, and I hope that he will wear it again."

At that time, Zduriencik said he had several telephone conversations with Griffey's agent, Brian Goldberg, and "probably would talk again."

Club president Chuck Armstrong went to Pebble Beach, California, to meet with Junior and judge his interest in coming back to the Mariners. It was a good meeting. But spring training opened in Peoria, Arizona, without Griffey.

The drama increased daily as word got out that Griffey was torn between signing with the Mariners or the Atlanta Braves, a team that would allow Junior to be closer to his Orlando home during spring training and the regular season.

The *Atlanta Journal-Constitution* reported on February 18 that Griffey had chosen the Braves, citing a source close to Junior. That was news to the Mariners brass.

I called Armstrong, and he doubted the accuracy of the report, because he had not heard from either Goldberg or Junior. Chuck knew that he would be among the first to know of Griffey's decision, one way or the other.

As the beat writers were busy composing their stories in the pressroom, I decided to call Goldberg's cell phone.

He picked up after the first ring, and I asked him about the *Journal-Constitution* report.

"Hold on—I want you to talk to someone," Goldberg said.

Griffey was on the phone, telling me that the report was wrong. He had not yet made up his mind.

"We are still kicking things around with my family and have not made a decision," Griffey said. "This is the first time in my career that I have been a free agent, and it's nerve-wracking."

He called it a difficult decision, because "I love Seattle." But the Braves offered him a chance to stay closer to home.

"You know how close I am to my wife and kids," he said.

After making sure Junior's comments were on the record, I returned to the pressroom, wrote my story, and sent it to my producer. When the story was posted on MLB.com, I turned to John Hickey, sitting next to me, and said, "You won't believe who I just interviewed."

He did not guess Griffey.

I told him of the conversation I had with Griffey and said the story was up and running on the MLB.com website.

Hickey rewrote his story.

Geoff Baker, sitting several seats away, overheard my conversation with Hickey. "[Griffey] is lying to you," he said. "I have two sources in Atlanta that tell me the Braves deal is done."

I thought, *In that case, write your story the way you want to write it. Who am I to stop you and your paper from looking foolish?*

I am sure several *Times* readers went to bed that night believing that Griffey was going to play for the Braves.

Times sports columnist Steve Kelley, who I have great respect for, wrote a column lamenting how the Mariners organization allowed Junior to slip away.

After spending the next day at the sports complex and getting no official word on Griffey's situation, I received a phone call from Brian Goldberg at around 5:00 p.m.

"Junior is coming back," Brian said.

My first call was to Bill Hill, the MLB.com west region editor, to give him the news. I wrote a story as quickly as I could to get it up on our website. General Manager Jack Zduriencik, meanwhile, called a press conference for 6:00 p.m. at the team's practice facility.

"I can't begin to tell you how ecstatic all of us are," Zduriencik said. "He is as well. I spoke to Brian a few minutes ago, and he said that Ken is relieved and excited about coming back to Seattle."

Griffey agreed to a one-year deal calling for a $2 million base salary and another $2.5 million in incentives.

He was worth every penny of it.

First-year manager Don Wakamatsu was leery at first to have Junior on his team, because he was worried that Griffey would want—and get—too much attention. But he signed off on the deal and welcomed the iconic outfielder with open arms.

The regular season started with Griffey in the lineup—but without Ichiro.

For the first time in his MLB career, Ichiro was placed on the fifteen-day disabled list because of a bleeding ulcer that apparently was related to the pressure the right fielder had put on himself during the World Baseball Classic that spring.

The late start did not prevent Ichiro from setting an MLB record with nine consecutive two-hundred-hit seasons, reaching that mark on September 13. Meanwhile, the Mariners became just the thirteenth team in MLB history to have a winning record following a hundred-plus-loss season.

Ace right-hander Felix Hernandez won his nineteenth game in the final game of the season, and the team celebrated its eighty-fifth win by carrying Junior and Ichiro off the field on their shoulders. It was an amazing sight for a team that did not compete for a playoff berth, but the season itself was a tremendous amount of fun for everyone including the media.

Ken Griffey Jr. was a big reason for that. He brought smiles back to the clubhouse, keeping everyone loose with his upbeat attitude and love of the game. Mike Sweeney also contributed greatly to the much-improved clubhouse atmosphere.

Junior ended his twenty-first big-league season with a .214 batting average, nineteen home runs, fifty-seven RBIs, and a team-high sixty-three walks. Most of his 387 at bats and 454 plate appearances came as the designated hitter.

"It was probably the most nervous and emotional roller coaster I have ever been on as a ballplayer," he said of his final at bat. "You never know when it will be your last."

A teary-eyed Griffey said he wasn't sure about his future.

"I am going to go back to Florida, talk to my family, and decide what is best for all of us."

For the first time since the '03 season, when the Mariners were in the hunt for a playoff spot, the '09 season was fun for me—mostly because of Griffey. He acted like the Kid back in 1989, smiling most of the time and joking with teammates, writers, and anyone else whom he came in contact with.

One Griffey moment that I'll always remember occurred at Dodger Stadium. Radio reporter Shannon Drayer, Larry Stone, and I were in the visiting clubhouse chatting with Junior. Suddenly, Griffey stops in midsentence, looks at Stoney, and says, "Is your shirt inside out?

Stoney looked, and yes, indeed, it was inside out. Neither Shannon nor I had noticed, because, frankly, it wasn't that obvious. But Junior noticed, and we all got a great laugh out of it—even Stoney. Of all the years I covered Junior, 2009 just might have been the best.

The season was a success in many ways, and my year perked up considerably in September. The Mariners were in Anaheim for a series against the Angels when I received a phone call from my son, Scott. He wanted me to meet his girlfriend, Emily Allardyce, at a bagel shop in Newport Beach, California.

We met up, had lunch, and spent about an hour or so chatting. Emily was a charming, beautiful, and down-to-earth attorney.

As I drove away, I called Becky and told her, "I just met Scott's future wife."

I'm not sure she believed me, but Dad's intuition proved to be right on the money. The romance blossomed, and they had an engagement dinner near San Diego in February 2010, the day before the Super Bowl.

Chapter 34

2010: The End of a Long Road

As good as the 2009 season was, the 2010 season was just the opposite.

I decided during the off-season that 2010 would be my final season as the Mariners reporter for MLB.com. It would be my fortieth year as a sportswriter, a career that consumed parts of five decades.

The job was getting harder, the travel was more difficult thanks in large part to the terrorist attacks nine years earlier, and I wanted to spend more time with my family.

Not only that, but I was beginning to feel like Inspector Gadget. Social media was running rampant in my profession, and for any given interview, I carried a notepad and pen, a camera, a Flip camera, a tape recorder, and a Blackberry cell phone that had to be turned on at all times. My life was dominated by blogs and tweets during the day and lack of sleep at night.

Our motto at MLB.com was "Write when you are awake, and think about what you are going to write next when you are asleep."

One of the advantages of the Internet is there are no limitations on how much you can write. One of the disadvantages of the Internet is there are no limitations on how much you write. The best way to drive Internet traffic is to constantly post new material on the website, and I don't know of anyone who does that better than MLB.com.

I also had a hunch that 2010 would be Ken Griffey Jr.'s last season, and I thought it was kind of cool to be retiring at the same time as

Junior, who had been such a huge part of my twenty-two years on the Mariners beat.

It never entered my mind that Junior's final year would be so short.

Griffey needed a little more than a month after the fun-filled 2009 season ended to decide whether to play one more season. On November 11, 2009, ten days before Junior's fortieth birthday, the Mariners announced that Griffey had signed a one-year contract.

"We all realize what he meant to the team on and off the field," General Manager Jack Zduriencik said. "His leadership was special. He's excited about coming back, and we're excited to have him back. He's a great guy, a fun guy, loves life, loves baseball, and loves the community. It's a real bonus for us to have him back."

The feeling was mutual.

"I'd like to thank the Mariners organization for inviting me back to play in 2010," Griffey said. "While 2009 was an awesome experience for me, my ultimate goal is for the Mariners to get to and win the World Series. To that end, I look forward to contributing in any role that [manager] Don [Wakamatsu] sees fit on the field and any manner I possibly can off the field."

Mariners fans were thrilled, and the acquisition of star left-handed starting pitcher Cliff Lee from the Phillies via a trade made the feel-good vibes feel even better. Zduriencik even unloaded overpriced and overweight pitcher Carlos Silva, trading him to the Chicago Cubs for outfielder Milton Bradley.

The pieces were in place for the Mariners to make a run at the playoffs.

So we thought.

Bradley, regarded throughout the industry as a problem child, showed up with a smile on his face. He seemed happy.

Griffey told me that if nothing else, his new teammate would "have a lot of fun here."

The first time I asked Bradley for an interview, he said, "Get out of my face!"

The second time I asked him for an interview, he unloaded a verbal tirade that included too many *f*-bombs to count. He would be pleasant one minute, giving Gregg Bell of the Associated Press a terrific interview, and then blow off another writer minutes later. It was like dealing with a schizophrenic.

Griffey and veteran Mike Sweeney, one of the nicest people ever to put on a major-league uniform, were just the opposite of Bradley. They were upbeat and kept everyone else—except for Milton—loose and upbeat as well.

Bradley's erratic behavior raised a red flag. So did a foot injury to Cliff Lee, suffered while he was going through a precamp throwing session. It would set him back for most of the spring.

The Mariners, minus Lee, treaded water for the first month of the regular season, posting an 11–12 record through April. An eight-game losing streak, which started on April 30 and ended on May 9, sent Seattle into a skid that catapulted the team to another horrible season.

On May 6, Bradley was placed on the restricted list for mental issues. Bradley, involved in numerous incidents on and off the field during his career, had requested help after leaving the team while a game against the Rays was still being played at Safeco Field.

An angry exchange with manager Don Wakamatsu following a strikeout in the sixth inning preceded Bradley's departure. The troubled outfielder would miss two weeks of the season as he underwent treatment.

But that was just the tip of the iceberg.

Five days after Bradley left the team, the Mariners went on a three-city road trip to Baltimore, Tampa Bay, and Oakland with a new hitting coach. Alan Cockrell was fired on Mother's Day, replaced by Alonzo Powell.

Griffey, epitomizing the overall team hitting slump, was batting .200 with no home runs and six RBIs after his first eighty at bats. There were rumblings that Junior might be talked into retiring or, heaven forbid, released from his contract.

As he waited for his flight from Seattle to Baltimore, Larry LaRue of the *Tacoma News-Tribune* worked on some Griffey-related notes that he had been gathering for a future story. Two unidentified players had told LaRue that Junior had been napping in the clubhouse during a recent game.

Upon hearing, "This is the final boarding call for flight …" LaRue shut down his computer, but instead of hitting Save, he accidentally hit the Publish button. The notes were now on the TNT website in the form of a blog. Larry Stone of the *Seattle Times* was one of the first to see the blog, read the blog, and react to the blog.

With LaRue in the air and unreachable, someone on the TNT sports staff rearranged the notes to make it read like a story, which it wasn't. When LaRue landed in Baltimore and turned on his cell phone, there were an unusual number of messages. Call the desk! Call the sports editor! Call, call, call.

The blog went viral, and it was a horrible time for him. It probably was his worst day since suffering a massive heart attack the previous year.

LaRue went to the ballpark the following night for the Mariners' series opener against the Orioles and walked into a room full of cold shoulders. In a pregame players-only meeting, they had decided to boycott LaRue before, during, and after games.

That is the worst possible scenario for a reporter.

Manager Don Wakamatsu denied that Griffey had been asleep in the clubhouse when he might have been used as a pinch hitter for catcher Rob Johnson in the ninth inning.

"What I know is that he was not sleeping when that situation came up, and I know that for a fact," Wakamatsu said. "When you read stuff, the first thing you think is *Is there any truth to it?* He was in the dugout. I said in my postgame press conference, when asked if he was available … I said yes. He was not sleeping.

"There are things you read, and people associated with the team know what the truth is. My statement is he was available to hit and no, he was not sleeping. I know that for a fact. Griff is trying to pull up evidence now in the TV footage."

Griffey called me over to his locker, where he was sitting on a chair.

"Look at this," he said, showing me a message on his cell phone.

It was a text from his wife, Melissa, saying that their teenage son, Trey, had been taken to an Orlando, Florida, hospital with a shoulder injury. Several of Trey's classmates had chided him for his dad's "nap." Trey finally had enough and got into a fight with two classmates.

Junior was near tears as he responded to the text message.

Luckily, Trey's shoulder injury did not require surgery, but the relationship between Lash and Griffey was severed.

Back in the press box, LaRue spent virtually the entire game working on a story explaining what had happened. His office would not allow him to write the truth, because, he was told, it would make the newspaper look bad. People make mistakes, and LaRue made a big one—but it wasn't intentional.

I kept him up to date on the game and provided some quotes for his game story.

We walked back to our respective hotels together, and I told him, "Well, at least the season is almost over."

He didn't laugh. It was May 11.

I was supposed to return to Seattle after the Orioles series, missing a three-game series against the Rays in St. Petersburg, and rejoin the team in Oakland. My travel plans changed. I went to Florida and had an interview with Junior.

I asked him if he had thought about retiring.

"I haven't gotten to that point," he said. "What would it take? I don't know. I haven't thought about anything but coming here and getting ready for a game."

The forty-year-old said he thought there still was some fuel left in his tank.

"If I didn't feel that I could compete, then why would I show up?" he said. "Why would I take early batting practice? Why would I take batting practice, period? That's just the way it is. I'm not there yet. I will figure that out when I get there, but I'm not there."

There came about two weeks later—on June 2.

Junior issued a farewell statement through the organization via a press release distributed to the Seattle-based media:

> I've come to a decision today to retire from Major
> League Baseball as an active player. This has been on
> my mind recently, but it's not an easy decision to come
> by. I am extremely thankful for the opportunity to have

played Major League Baseball for so long and thankful for all of the friendships I have made, while also being proud of my accomplishments.

I'd like to thank my family for all of the sacrifices they have made all of these years for me. I'd like to thank the Seattle Mariners organization for allowing me to finish my playing career where it started. I look forward to a continued, meaningful relationship with them for many years to come.

While I feel I am still able to make a contribution on the field, and nobody in the Mariners front office has asked me to retire, I told the Mariners when I met with them prior to the 2009 season and was invited back, that I will never allow myself to become a distraction. I feel that without enough occasional starts to be sharper coming off the bench, my continued presence as a player would be an unfair distraction to my teammates, and their success as team is what the ultimate goal should be.

My hope is that my teammates can focus on baseball and win a championship for themselves and for the great fans of Seattle, who so very much deserve one. Thanks to all of you for welcoming me back, and thanks again to everyone over the years that has played a part in the success of my career.

He drove east from Seattle back to his home in Orlando. The season continued without him.

When the final out of the season was made on October 3 against the Athletics at Safeco Field (a fifth straight Seattle loss), the Mariners limped out of the quiet clubhouse with a 61–101 record.

During the seventh inning of my final game on the beat, a cake was delivered to the press box along with some champagne. The cake was compliments of Ken Griffey Jr.

I called and thanked him.

The Mariners organization had a farewell message put up on the video screen, which I thought was a nice touch. Several players saw it and wished me good luck and much fun in retirement.

I found it an odd coincidence that the first major-league team I covered, the Athletics in 1971, won 101 games, and the last team I covered, the 2010 Mariners, lost 101 games.

Thanks to T. R. Sullivan, the beat reporter for the AL West champion Texas Rangers, and Bill Hill, the MLB.com's west regional editor, I was on the team that covered the best-of-five division series between the Rangers and Rays. TR, who had delivered the *Mercury-News* at Ft. Ord, California, when I covered the Athletics in the early '70s, requested that I be his wingman for the AL division series.

With Hill leading the way, a team that also included Lyle Spencer, Ian Browne, Bill Chastain, and Rhett Bollinger worked hard during the series. It was the frosting on the cake for me.

My last day on the job was October 31. For some reason, I figured Halloween would be the perfect day to ride off into the sunset.

But my game plan was altered a bit on November 10, when I received a phone call from the Mariners public relations department that Hall of Fame announcer Dave Niehaus had died of a massive heart attack while preparing for a barbeque at his Bellevue home.

It seemed like a fitting conclusion to a season filled with despair and disappointment.

Chapter 35

2011–2014: Golf Takes Center Stage

My game plan entering the retirement years of my life was to do some part-time work for MLB.com but mostly focus on spending more time with my wife and family along with getting my golf handicap down to a respectable number.

We learned early the previous year that Scott and Emily were going to get married in Edinburgh, Scotland, not far from Nairn, where her dad, mother-in-law, and grandfather lived. Emily visited Scotland often as a child and always dreamed of getting married there. We thought it was a great idea.

Becky and I had been planning a retirement trip to Europe, specifically to Italy, Austria, and perhaps Switzerland. We changed our plans, opting instead for Barcelona, where Becky's son, Brad, spent a semester of his college; London; and then Scotland. It would be a trip of a lifetime topped off by the wedding. We had no idea that the nuptials would be so extravagant.

The part-time gig with MLB.com lasted from the first week of January to the end of spring training. I was not ready to spend that much time writing, so I resigned.

The trip to Europe was fantastic. Becky and I enjoyed every minute of the journey, and the fact that her son was part of Scott's wedding party made it even more special. He stayed with us at Marriott's Dalmahoy Golf Resort for a week. We played golf there a couple of times, and those games were good bonding sessions.

Scott set up a two-day golf excursion with five of his wedding-party guests to other courses including North Berwick, Lunden, and Lunden Links. We hoped to play the Old Course at St. Andrews and spent the night in St. Andrews, but there were no tee times available. That was a bit of a bummer.

However, Brad decided to take a cab from our hotel at 2:00 a.m. and wait in line at the Old Course, hoping to get on. He explained to the starter that his brother was getting married in Edinburgh later in the day and he had to be back by three o'clock. Brad got the first tee time of the day and played the most memorable round of golf in his young life.

Becky and I toured the old city the way tourists tour old cities: taking numerous pictures.

For our part, the wedding went off without a hitch. Becky and I hosted the rehearsal dinner for eighty-some people, and a good time was had by all. There was dinner and dancing and meeting Emily's relatives, some of whom had traveled all the way from New Zealand to attend.

The St. Giles Church is spectacular and the setting could not have been more glamorous. The reception, held at the Balmoral Hotel, was something out of a Hollywood movie, complete with a bagpiper and Scottish announcer.

A little more than ten months after the amazing wedding ceremony in Edinburgh, Andrew Thomas Irving Street was born at Cesars-Sinai Hospital in Los Angeles. As it turned out, I was in Pasadena at the time of Andrew's arrival on April 29, 2012. He held out a couple of weeks, perhaps because he wanted to make sure his grandpa was in town when he had his coming-out party.

When we returned from Europe, my two best friends, Bob Sherwin and Kirby Arnold, decided to start a golf website called GolfersWest. com. The goal was to list every golf course from Colorado to Hawaii and play as many of them as we could.

Bob provided all of the financing, and the two of us, along with Zach, the webmaster, designed what we think was a terrific-looking site. It debuted in the spring of 2012. Since then, we have played several rounds and written about our experiences. Bob took his son, Bobby, to

Scotland in March and wrote a series of superb stories about some of the oldest golf courses in the world.

I stuck to the United States, writing articles about Coeur d'Alene in Idaho, which has the only floating green in the world; Sunriver, Oregon; and Strawberry Farms in Irvine, California, a round of golf set up by Scott and a couple of his buddies.

Bob and I spent a week in Florida in December of 2012 and began 2013 with a weeklong trip to Kauai, the northernmost island in Hawaii, playing such great layouts as Makai, Prince, Kauai Lagoons, and Poipu Bay.

Between the website and being members of the Northwest Golf Media Association, there is enough golf to be played to keep us busy and out of trouble.

I still attend baseball games occasionally. I am a lifetime member of the BBWAA, which allows me to go to any regular-season game anywhere in the major leagues for free and also vote for the Hall of Fame. I hope to take Becky to Cooperstown, New York someday. If she doesn't understand why baseball has meant so much to me for most of my life, she will definitely understand after visiting the Hall of Fame.

In the meantime, the game plan is to hit as many golf balls as straight and as far as possible; work on being a good husband, father, and grandfather; and enjoy the future as I have enjoyed the great majority of the past.

Index

G

Tom Gage 74
Terry Galvin 36
Ross Game 4
Freddy Garcia 119, 149
Claude Gilbert 47
Pat Gillick 139, 146, 149–150
Chris Gobrecht 86
Mike Goff 94
Brian Goldberg 44, 126–127, 174, 176–177
Ron Goldman 92
Juan Gonzalez 107–108
Slade Gorton 84
Dave Graybill 96
Dick Green 18–19, 51, 189
Ken Griffey Jr. 44, 59, 67, 72–73, 76, 80, 85, 87, 93, 97, 102, 106–107, 109, 124, 126, 129, 137, 143, 158, 167, 171, 174–175, 178, 180, 185
Ken Griffey Sr. 44, 59, 78
Lee Guetterman 60
Carlos Guillen 119, 151
Jose Guillen 166, 170, 172
Ken Gurnick 126–127, 135, 160
Fred Guzman 42

H

Chris Haft 161
John Halama 119
Tonya Harding 110
Mike Hargrove 107, 157, 166–168
Mike Harkey 59
Gene Harris 74
Shigetoshi Hasegawa xi, 147–148
Bill Haselman 89
Ron Hassey 168
Mike Heath 77
Mike Hegan 18
Dave Henderson 54, 56
Rickey Henderson 42, 60, 99

George Hendrick 16
Cathy Henkel 110, 138, 160
Felix Hernandez 166, 171, 178
Tim Hevly 127–128
John Hickey 108, 153, 163, 176–177
Tom Hicks 167
Bill Hill 177, 186
Marlyn Hines 1
Brian Holman 57, 74, 82
Jerome Holtzman 25
Ken Holtzman 17
Bob Hope 6
Art Howe 107
Dan Howitt 88
Paul Hoynes 151
Dan Hruby 37
Catfish Hunter 12, 17–18, 23, 25
Saddam Hussein 147

I

Raul Ibanez 170, 175
John Imbach 5

J

Mike Jackson 82, 84
Reggie Jackson 9, 12, 14, 17, 22–23, 65, 73, 132
Bruce Jenkins 34
Deron Johnson 17, 54
Randy Johnson xii, 74, 77, 81, 85, 87, 91, 100, 106, 111–112, 116, 119, 130
Rob Johnson 183
Adam Jones 170–171
Roger Jongewaard 59
Michael Jordan 110

K

Gary Kaseff 77
Mike Keck 2
Steve Kelley 177

193

Mike Warren 42, 119, 136
Dan Wartelle 128, 136
Jarrod Washburn 171
Gene Washington 28
Herb Washington 24–25
Mike West 7
John Wetteland 98
Jack White 38
Delvin Williams 28
Dick Williams 12–13, 16, 18, 20, 23,
    55–56, 68, 71, 117, 130, 146
Dan Wilson 88, 91
Marc Wilson 37
Randy Winn 146

James Witherell 3
Chet Wood 27
Woody Woodward 69, 71, 81, 83–84,
    87–88, 97

Y

Hiroshi Yamauchi 84
Matt Young 54

Z

Jack Zduriencik 175–177, 181